Better Writers

Applying new findings about grammar and technical accuracy

Debra Myhill

Better Writers by Debra Myhill

© Courseware 2001

British Library Cataloguing-in-Publication Data. ISBN 1 898 737 24 X

INTRODUCTION

In the course of the last five years there have been massive changes in the expectations placed upon English teachers and their pupils. The changes have included the introduction of the National Literacy Strategy (NLS) in primary schools, a new national curriculum for English, revised national tests at key stages 2 and 3, and new examinations at GCE and GCSE levels. Now, a further initiative will affect Key Stage 3 with the introduction into secondary schools of the model of language and the pedagogy espoused by the National Literacy Strategy.

Test results, the government's preferred yardstick, have indicated for some years that major improvements have been achieved in the quality of children's reading abilities and, by and large, few teachers of English would disagree with this finding. However, this progress has not - apparently - been matched in writing and this, in turn, has led to concern that national standards are not rising and targets will not be met.

There could be many reasons for this. Some commentators and teachers argue that, perhaps unintentionally, the National Literacy Strategy places a greater emphasis on reading and makes reading more enjoyable for pupils than writing. Others argue that the teaching of writing has lagged behind reading for many years and that, while the experience of extended writing for many pupils is limited to diaries and stories the assessment focus has been on spelling, grammar and neatness rather than on structure and communicative success.

It has also been suggested that too much is expected from boys' writing at Key Stage 1, when their motor-skills are insufficiently developed and that the clear water between their performances and those of girls at this key stage sets a pattern for their schooling that persists. Finally, to complicate the picture, and as later sections suggest, the 'problem' of boys' writing may relate to perception as well as performance.

So, for a number of reasons, there has been a renewed research emphasis on writing and on the development of writing skills and, in theory at least, it is the findings from this research which should go on to underpin the new Key Stage 3 Framework and strategy in secondary schools. However, as teachers know, the reality is that strategies have a tendency to water down research findings and to gloss over their subtleties. Therefore, this book represents a serious attempt to outline recent developments in the teaching of writing and to see how they can be applied to good practice in secondary schools.

Learning how to write is at once one of the most commonplace and one of the most complex activities we ask children to undertake in school. The next section in this book illustrates how the teaching of writing has developed over the past thirty years or so, and it is hoped that the ideas and thinking underlying what is said here will build on the best of current practice. The emphasis upon language and linguistic characteristics is an attempt to redress an imbalance and it is not our intention that the strategies in this book should replace all that has gone before – rather we hope these strategies will enhance, focus and strengthen current good practice. However, the time is ripe for the linguistic features of writing to be given due weight alongside the literary features of writing, and for teaching to address more explicitly the skills, techniques and attributes of 'good' writing.

In that sense, this book goes beyond the Key Stage 3 strategy and the retraining of teachers. Instead, it offers thinking and reflective practitioners avenues to explore which can develop their professional skills and build on the existing base of their professional expertise. Some of the book's findings will surprise even the most experienced classroom teachers but the classroom suggestions and ideas will enable all teachers to investigate the variety of ways in which children can become, in the words of the title, Better Writers.

The title is apt. Our focus is upon the *writer* and how the writer may be enabled to understand how to improve his or her writing, and to recognise the characteristics which contribute to that success. In so many of the weaker pieces of writing with which all English teachers are familiar, there is a voice cramped and silenced by an inability to communicate effectively. It is not that weak writers have nothing to say: it is that they lack confidence in how to say it. For writers of all abilities, greater assurance in crafting, shaping, selecting and polishing the words and structures they create is an important step in helping them to find their writing voices.

Debra Myhill

INDEX

1   HOW WE GOT HERE

The last forty years have witnessed more significant changes in attitudes towards the teaching of the writing than in any preceding era. Many of those changes have been mirrored in the teaching of reading and the interpretation of text, and also more widely in altered cultural and sociological values. It seems salient, therefore, to open a book which looks at how we might sharpen and refine the way we teach writing in the future with a brief retrospect. Knowing where we have been helps us to understand where we are going!

The kinds of writing which dominated English teaching before the 1960s were the formal composition and the discursive essay. Indeed, the composition was for many years used as the basis for judgements about selection to grammar schools or to independent education. The emphasis was placed clearly on the writing product, not upon the processes which writers use to arrive at the product while written work was marked (and formally assessed) for the extent of its accuracy in spelling, punctuation and grammatical construction.

However, growing dissatisfaction with this product-based approach to writing at a time when there was a broader assertion of liberal ideas prompted the emergence of a new rationale for writing. This valued the child's own voice and recognised how writing develops from initial ideas to the final, polished piece. A substantial shift occurred in the types of writing task being set, with young writers being encouraged to express their feelings in their writing and to write from personal experience. The work of Donald Graves in America reinforced this stress upon the authentic voice of the child and added to it by suggesting that unless children understood the processes of writing then it was impossible for them to have full ownership of the product. He also advocated one-to-one conferencing where the teacher allowed the child to discover what he or she really wanted to write and helped the child to develop the writing skills to accomplish it.

In practice, of course, few teachers had the opportunity to run one-to-one conferences and the examination system inevitably focused teachers' minds upon the product of writing, as well as the process. But Graves' ideas, synthesised through teacher training and a new wave of English textbooks, have had a major impact. The words 'drafting' and 'editing' have entered the discourse of the English classroom and many – some might say, too many - writing tasks set both in primary and secondary schools invite children to write from their own experience.

Critics of this approach to writing have levelled two substantial criticisms against it. Firstly, the role of the teacher is reduced from being an active instructor or guide to being a 'facilitator' who enables the child to write but offers little in the way of direct guidance. Secondly, critics have maintained that the reliance on the child's own voice privileges advantaged, middle class children whose 'own voice' also happens to be that of many of the written discourses which the educational system values. The absence of active teaching of writing and the emphasis on a personal voice disenfranchises those children who do not already have access to the dominant discourse. Many English teachers will remember writing primary school diaries where they embellished their personal experiences in order to deliver the writing type that the teacher applauded! Others in the class – deemed to be and ultimately less successful - may not have mastered this strategy.

In the 1980s, and partly as a response to these concerns, an approach to the teaching of writing emerged which placed considerable emphasis upon the different genres of writing. In contrast to process approaches to writing, highlighting genre awarded more significance to explicit teaching about the characteristics of different genres. The rationale was that by helping writers to understand and imitate different genres they would learn how to access the dominant genres of our culture – a rationale of empowerment through demystifying different forms of writing. Beverley Derewianka's (1996) work on genres such as procedure, recount, explanation, report and so on are now familiar through the work of Wray and Lewis (1997), particularly in their use of writing frames. In practical terms, the impact of the genre approach can often be seen most clearly in the types of writing task set and, at its worst, is reduced to the use of a genre as a vehicle for generating writing about reading. In English examination coursework, the preponderance of newspaper articles, and letters and diaries written in role are prime examples of how this latter outcome has impacted on teaching.

What can be said about the future? Both the process and genre approaches to writing are acknowledged by the English National Curriculum in its latest (Curriculum 2000) version. There is an increasing level of reference to the skills of drafting and editing, particularly in Key Stage 2. At Key Stages 3 and 4, children are expected to develop their ability to 'plan, draft, redraft and proof-read their work on paper and on screen' and it is also expected that they will be taught 'how techniques, structures, forms and styles vary' in their study of reading.

The curriculum and also the draft Framework for English years 7-9, maintain the emphasis on purpose, form and audience. At GCSE, the specification of the four groups of writing which all candidates must cover is a direct reflection of genre approaches to writing. Slightly confusingly, the National Literacy Strategy also makes considerable use of Derewianka's work on genre, adopting her six text types (including, instruction, report, recount and persuasive texts) within a different model. There is more on working within genre in Section 13.

If there is any shift in emphasis here, it is in the direction of discussing 'forms' of writing. The notes appended to the curriculum remind us that *forms are adapted to the writer's aim and the intended reader*. This is why the two key questions a writer needs to ask are 'Who am I writing for?' and 'Why am I writing?' Framed by these two questions, the form is a less fixed medium and indeed some writers may deliberately manipulate form for a specific effect – such as a persuasive argument conveyed through an emotive letter from an imaginary character, or an information leaflet presented as a dialogue between two people on the relevant topic.

What these differing approaches to writing mean in terms of writing types and teacher activities is summarised in the chart overleaf. It provides a rough and ready guide to the status quo as it was before national assessment and the most recent research brought a new focus on this area.

In the longer term, writing is set to undergo further transformation. If almost all writing is initiated on screen, using templates for writing and grammar and spell checkers, and, increasingly, dictation rather than a keyboard for input there may be an increasing overlap between writing and talk. At the same time 'instant' interactive screen writing (chatrooms, text messages and the next generation of mobile telephones) is likely to put pressure on writing and notions of written correctness. And, as usual, education will undoubtedly be playing 'catch-up'!

A SUMMARY OF DIFFERENT APPROACHES TO THE TEACHING OF WRITING

APPROACH	TEACHER...	WRITING TYPES
Product	◆ sets writing task and awaits its completion ◆ uses grades or numbers in marking ◆ corrects all mistakes ◆ looks especially for correctness in spelling, punctuation and grammar	◆ written composition in response to a brief title ◆ discursive essay on a controversial topic ◆ literary critical response ◆ general preference for the third person voice
Process	◆ helps initiate ideas for writing task ◆ talks about the process of writing, especially drafting ◆ may mark drafts as work in progress ◆ uses written comments or oral feedback in response to writing ◆ corrects mistakes selectively ◆ looks at communicative content as well as surface accuracy	◆ personal writing, including autobiographical pieces ◆ creative writing, including poetry ◆ considerable use of first person voice ◆ unfinished pieces as well as completed pieces
Genre	◆ sets writing tasks within conventional genre categories ◆ may use reading texts as models of genre ◆ draws writers' attention to audience ◆ may provide real audiences for writing ◆ assesses use of genre features when marking ◆ looks at ability to recreate genre as well as surface accuracy	◆ genre writing types, especially ◆ newspaper reports, ◆ diaries, ◆ letters, ◆ information leaflets, ◆ advertisements or promotional material.

2 HOW TO DEVELOP WRITING SKILLS

Why might the process and genre approaches to writing outlined in the previous section be relevant to our thinking about how to create better writers as well as being the starting point for change? The fundamental reason is that underlying both approaches are strong philosophies, or models, of what English teaching is for and, of course, what writing is for. Using the familiar models proposed by Brian Cox, it is possible to see that the process approach is rooted in a personal growth model and that the genre approach is rooted in the cultural analysis model.

It would be easy to go on to argue that, in the process approach, writing is used as a tool to develop the writer, giving him or her a voice and allowing inner feelings and thoughts to be given expression and validity. The teacher is an enabler of the child's personal growth and self-awareness, rather than being in any way instrumental in developing the child's writing. Likewise, the genre approach inducts writers into the dominant genres of our culture, inviting writers to imitate and replicate the available genres. The emphasis is upon the form of the genre, much less upon its linguistic features, and writers are much more likely to be set the task of writing in a particular genre than to study explicitly the linguistic characteristics of that genre. What this indicates is that what both approaches (and, indeed, also the earlier product approach to writing) have in common is that they are stronger on why children are writing than on how to help them become better writers.

There is a good reason for this. While much media and professional attention has been devoted to controversies over how reading is taught, debate concerning how writing should be taught has been strangely mute. Much of our professional attention as teachers has been directed towards the kinds of writing tasks we set – towards drawing on the child's experiences or establishing appropriate audiences and purposes for writing. In summary, teachers have - at different times - overemphasised correctness, overemphasised personal response, and overemphasised form. Although there has been much valuable work on how to mark and assess children's writing, there has been almost no attention given to how to intervene during writing and how to be active in teaching writing. Put simply, we set up writing tasks and we mark writing, but we do little to help writers understand how to write better.

That may be because there has been a theoretical void at the heart of both the process and genre approaches to writing. They are both seen as practical strategies to provide the contexts within which pupils will bring commitment and variety to their writing. So, where textbooks and examination guides have endeavoured to unpack the features of, for example, reporting or advertisements they have slipped into stereotypical accounts and produced advice which is countered by examples of successful and varied practice.

The outcome has been that in spite of public concern over reading standards, it is writing which is the least well-managed aspect of the English curriculum. At every key stage and at GCSE, children are likely to achieve higher marks for reading than for writing. And, accordingly, If overall standards in English are to improve, it is in writing that the most significant improvements will need to be made.

This is well understood in some quarters. The extension of the National Literacy Strategy into Key Stage 3 and the introduction of voluntary national assessment tests by the Qualifications and Curriculum Authority (QCA) for years 7 and 8 represents a strategic attempt to address literacy but, especially, writing. The issue of boys' performance in English relative to girls is currently high on the government's agenda and is a concern for many schools and here, again, it would seem to be writing which has be addressed if the achievement gap is to be narrowed.

In the 1999 Key Stage 2 tests, the overall performance of boys at level 4 increased by 14%, considerably narrowing the gap with girls but, in writing, whilst almost two-thirds of girls achieved level 4, only 49% of boys managed to do likewise. In response to these results, John Stannard, then the director of the National Literacy Strategy, acknowledged that although the literacy hour appeared to have significantly improved boys' achievements, 'the biggest challenge was raising standards in writing'. The article from which this quotation is taken was published in the *Times Educational Supplement* in October 1999. In the article, reproduced overleaf, Geraldine Hackett, sums up the wider public concern about this situation at that time and since.

The reasons for the gap between achievements in reading and writing are, on one level at least, straightforward: children have an understanding of vocabulary and language structures which they can recognise and understand when encountering reading texts but which they are unable to draw upon when writing for themselves. In other words, passive linguistic competence needs to become active linguistic competence in order to facilitate effective writing, and implicit knowledge about language needs to become explicit.

Boys close reading gap but still trail in writing

BOYS in their final year are rapidly catching up with girls at reading, but more than half are still not able to write at the level expected of 11-year-olds.

The latest analysis of national test results shows that in the last year the reading scores of boys have shot up by 14 percentage points, narrowing the gender gap.

While girls are now only six percentage points ahead in reading, they retain their substantial lead in writing – almost two thirds of them achieve the required level, compared with 49 per cent of boys.

However, ministers recognise that to reach English targets set for 2002, standards in writing among boys will have to improve. Funds are being provided to train all teachers of 10 and 11-year-olds in the teaching of writing.

John Stannard, director of the National Literacy Strategy, said boys seemed to have benefited from the concentration on guided reading during the literacy hour but the biggest challenge was raising standards in writing.

(TES, October 1999)

However, this is not the only reason why achievements in writing so often lag behind other aspects of language performance. Writing is routinely used as the medium for learning and for assessment at all stages of the educational system and, as such, it ceases to be the immediate focus of attention. Whilst the writing may well be corrected for superficial accuracy in spelling or punctuation, the principal assessment focus is concerned with the extent to which the writing indicates evidence, for example, of understanding of a literary text or a historical period. The sheer amount of writing children produce during their time in school has often been noted (see Sheeran and Barnes' work, for example), but only on rare occasions is the writing itself made the focus of teaching attention.

That may be about to change. The proposed Framework for Literacy in Years 7-9 establishes explicit teaching objectives which must be met within English teaching, and must be supported and reinforced across the curriculum. These relate more closely to writing and to language but, if their introduction is to be a success, they will have to be embedded into practice rather than bolted on to it. The same framework also brings the pedagogy of the National Literacy Strategy into secondary education and this may, in turn, increase the danger that the message which teachers receive implies that these aspects of language and writing should be fragmented and isolated in teaching.

That would be unfortunate. As this section indicates, and as many teachers recognise, there are weaknesses at a national level in the teaching of writing springing out of theoretical uncertainties and an overemphasis on correctness and presentation. An overt preoccupation with grammar has already shown itself to be a blind alley but the avenue represented by genre and form is a useful way out if it can be supported by and linked to close reference to features of text and language. Making those connections is the aim of the remainder of this book.

3 CLASSROOM PRACTICE 1

Auditing writing in English schemes of work

A worthwhile exercise for English teachers committed to helping children become better writers is to conduct an audit of their schemes of work or classroom practice. This allows an objective analysis of the nature of demands and the extent of opportunities for explicit teaching of writing.

It can be applied to the work undertaken by a primary school class, a tracked group in the secondary school or to aspects of a departmental or personal scheme of work. Using the pro forma (reproduced in completed form on the facing page but as a copymaster in Appendix 2), the teacher can then note down every occasion in which children are expected to write, including when the writing is a means to an end and not an end in itself.

This will include anything from note-taking, brainstorming, drafting ideas and writing down key points from group discussion to providing feedback to a whole class. The next step is to decide what the purpose of that writing was, what the teaching focus was for the circumstances in which the writing task was undertaken, and what aspects of learning were, or would be, assessed through the writing. If the writing is not assessed, because it was work in progress or preliminary notes for example, then the teacher can record 'not assessed'.

Auditing of this kind helps English departments and teachers to identify where, and when, writing is the focus of attention and to look at how the department might develop continuity and progression in the teaching of writing. It also allows departments to see whether one form of writing, such as narrative, receives more attention than other forms. This is likely to be the case. Because so much of English teaching is literature or reading-based, a considerable amount of writing in English is used to show understanding of reading as the sample audit overleaf, based on a class reader, illustrates. Over a key stage, it may be evident that most writing falls into this category and opportunities may need to be created to build in an explicit focus on writing into reading-focused schemes of work.

AN EXAMPLE OF A COMPLETED AUDIT

Title of Scheme of Work: 'Buddy' by Nigel Hinton (class reader)			Year Group: 8

Aims of Scheme of Work:

♦ to develop close reading skills, including analysis of authorial technique;
♦ to study differences between a book text and a TV text;
♦ to encourage confidence in reading beyond the literal.

Writing Task	Purpose	Teaching focus	What will be assessed?
Letter from Buddy to his absent mum.	To understand Buddy's feelings.	Reading	Reading beyond the literal
'The Croxley Street Murder' – narrative.	To recognise and replicate creation of suspense.	Writing	Ability to write in horror genre, creating suspense
Notes on racism and racist language	To understand anti-racist theme	Reading	Ability to identify racist references and author's viewpoint.
Script of sub-text at the parents' evening	To understand gap between what is said and what is thought.	Reading	Ability to understand meaning beyond the literal
Notes on why Buddy's dad is different	To understand theme of outsiders/social exclusion	Reading	Not assessed
Essay on Buddy's feelings towards his father	To understand relationships and themes in the novel	Reading	Ability to read beyond the literal, with close reference to the text
Total number of writing tasks: 6			Total number of tasks with explicit focus on writing skills 1

EVALUATION – The focus of the majority of writing tasks is on showing how well they have understood their reading, because the principal learning outcomes were reading-related. It is noticeable that there were many other writing tasks (not listed here) such as lists, spider diagrams, and charts which were used to help develop reading skills. Little explicit writing is taught. The creation of suspense in the horror narrative is explicitly taught building on the model found in 'Buddy'. Explicit attention to writing skills could usefully be built into the final essay.

4 THE MISTAKES STUDENTS MAKE

In 1996, QCA (then SCAA) commissioned an investigation into writing in GCSE English examinations. The Technical Accuracy Project (TAP) as it was called, spanned three years, culminating in a final report that was published by QCA in 1999 (*Technical Accuracy in writing in GCSE English: research findings*, QCA, 1999). There is a more detailed account of its work in Appendix 1.

The aim of the project was to develop a series of coding frames which would permit a detailed analysis of children's writing, and be useful to teachers of writing. The six frames investigated were concerned with the use of:

1. spelling;
2. punctuation;
3. Non-Standard English usage;
4. clause structure and word class usage;
5. paragraphing;
6. textual organisation.

In developing the frames, there was a commitment to investigating writing from several perspectives: from the word level (spelling) to sentence level (punctuation; clause analysis, non-Standard English) to whole text level (paragraphing; textual organisation). The analysed samples of pupils' work (taken from GCSE examination papers) were taken from both narrative and non-narrative text writing types to allow comparisons between the two. Overall, the investigation focused upon three characteristics of writing. These were:

- accuracy;
- effectiveness;
- patterns of usage.

Pupils' accuracy in spelling, in correct use of sentence punctuation, in paragraphing and in the use of non-Standard English was measured. Their effectiveness in handling clauses, in linking paragraphs, and in whole text features, such as cohesion and establishing a reader-writer relationship, was recorded. A final layer of analysis looked at patterns of usage of linguistic features and devices, such as commas, adjectives, and conjuncts to link paragraphs. So, precisely what kind of writing features did these coding frames explore and what did they reveal about pupil performances in terms of their accuracy, effectiveness and use? The chart on the facing page summarises the key features analysed under each of the frame headings. Then, the main findings related to each writing feature are discussed in more detail. The analysis distinguished the performances of writers at GCSE grades A, C and F which are translated here as the performances of the best, average and weakest writers.

SUMMARY OF WRITING FEATURES ANALYSED

1 SPELLING	2 PUNCTUATION	3 NON-STANDARD ENGLISH
<ul><li>accuracy</li><li>sophistication of vocabulary</li><li>error patterns</li><li>omissions</li><li>sound</li><li>endings</li></ul>	<ul><li>capital letter to begin sentences</li><li>full stop to end sentences</li><li>comma usage:</li><li>to demarcate clauses; to separate items in a list; parenthetic; splicing</li><li>It's/its confusions</li><li>omissive apostrophes</li><li>possessive apostrophes</li><li>speech marks</li><li>other punctuation devices: colon; semi-colon; dashes; brackets</li></ul>	<ul><li>irregular past tense/past participle forms</li><li>subject/verb agreement</li><li>adjectives used as adverbs</li><li>more with comparative adjective</li><li>use of prepositions</li><li>me with subject Noun Phrase</li><li>no plural marker on nouns of quantity, measurement &c</li><li>use of definite/indefinite article</li></ul>

4 CLAUSE STRUCTURE AND WORD CLASS USAGE	5 PARAGRAPHING	6 TEXTUAL ORGANISATION
<ul><li>sentence length and variety</li><li>co-ordinated clauses</li><li>subordinate clauses</li><li>pattern of use of: finite verbs; abstract nouns; adjectives; adverbs; non-lexical words</li></ul>	<ul><li>use of paragraphs</li><li>paragraphing of dialogue</li><li>linking devices</li><li>conjuncts</li><li>adverbials of time and place</li><li>linguistic patterning</li><li>structural patterning</li><li>topic sentences</li></ul>	<ul><li>openings</li><li>endings</li><li>reader-writer relationship</li><li>cohesion and coherence</li></ul>

1 SPELLING

Although accuracy in spelling predictably increases with overall performance as measured by a GCSE grade, there are interesting differences in the types of error made at each grade which have clear teaching implications. The best writers (those typically achieving Grade A for the subject) have largely mastered the letter patterns and sequences of English spelling and make errors which are highly plausible. In particular, they have trouble with double consonants in the middle of words, sometimes using a double where a single is required and vice versa. For example:

> *accross, ballance, dissapointed, adress, milennium,*

They also make errors in words where there is an unstressed vowel sound, although it is important to note that this is most likely to be in the context of complex or sophisticated vocabulary, rather than in simple words with an unstressed vowel. So, good writers are unlikely to spell *animal* as *anamal* or *garden* as *gardin,* but their errors did include:

> *definate, appatising, persistant, detinated, mollastation, domented*

A final problem category for good writers is that of word division. There is a tendency to split words which should be one word.

> *over heard, can not, sun light*

Occasionally, the reverse pattern is found where two words are written as one.

> *a lot, infact*

Writers whose performance might be considered to be average (typically achieving Grade C for the subject) tend to make spelling errors which are broadly similar to those of the best writers, but with some resemblance to those made by the weakest writers (typically at Grade F for the subject). The one pattern of error which seems to be particularly significant for the average writers is confusion over homophones.

> *hear/here, their/there, know/no*

The weakest writers, however, reveal major problems with spelling. Some of the spellings are not recognisable, even in the context, while others show considerable weaknesses in matching sounds and symbols.

sucsefally; oppion, vacanances, puninant

Difficulty in sequencing and ordering sound-symbol correspondences is evident in the number of spellings which have inversions and letter reversals.

beign, strenght, agianst, nevre, frielndy, hoilday

One other problem which is very much a feature of the weakest writers' spelling is the tendency to omit a letter or a syllable from the spelling. Whilst at higher grades, omission often leaves the sound of a word largely unaffected (*casulty, suvive*) for the weakest writers the omission substantially alters the sound of the word and is often only recognisable because of the context in which it is written.

finis[h]ed, clean[in]g, sta[n]d, happ[en]ing, physi[ca]lly

The link between examination grades and spelling abilities is not surprising given that accuracy is a criteria for success in the examination mark schemes and is often given particular weighting by examiners. However, the analysis does reveal that patterns of spelling weakness are not a set of points on a continuum and this, in turn, argues persuasively that the teaching of spelling should be targeted at pupils' spelling needs to be most effective. It also underlines just how severe problems with spelling can be for the weakest writers, many of whom are still struggling with the most basic competence of matching the letters on the page to the sound of the word.

2   PUNCTUATION

Marking sentences: Writers are much more likely to use a capital letter correctly to begin a sentence than they are to use a full stop to end one. This suggests that writers understand the conventions of sentence punctuation but may have more trouble recognising syntactically where a sentence ends. In other words, they know that a sentence begins with a capital letter and ends with a full stop but, in practice, although they are confident with capitalisation at the sentence start, they are less sure about what constitutes a sentence end. This uncertainty is exacerbated by the tendency to use a comma at a sentence end where a full stop is required (a comma splice). The two examples below show how the comma is used as a substitute for a full stop, splicing together two sentences.

> *Most people affected by homelessness are young people between the age of 16-25, some of the reasons are because their parents throw them out of home because they were too much for their parents to handle, they ran away from home because they couldn't live for another day under the same roof ...*

> *I went out on Wednesday night, just for a drink with the girls up the Bull's Head, there was only Ang, Lizzy, Amy and me but we had a good laugh. They had a Karaoke up the pub which was a laugh, we all went up on the stage and sang All Saints, 'Never Ever'...*

One difference between the average and the weakest writers is that although the comma splice is a feature of both grades, at the higher grade it accounts for the majority of errors in sentence punctuation. However, the weakest writers are highly likely to omit punctuation at the end of a sentence altogether. This suggests that, at or around the C grade level, teaching might usefully focus on the incorrect use of commas to splice together two sentences, whereas with pupils working towards lower grades more substantial work on sentence structure may be necessary.

The use of the comma: The analysis highlighted how the principal issue relating to the use of commas in writing is their relative sparseness. This may simply reflect changing trends in comma use nationally: many publishing houses now adopt a policy of using commas only where absolutely necessary. Certainly, where clarity of meaning is potentially at stake, GCSE writers at the higher grades tend to use commas. The occurrence of commas to separate items in a list and to demarcate clauses are the most common usages. In the work of the weakest writers, however, there is a significant dearth of commas (matched by the lack of full stops), underlining the fact that punctuation in general is clearly an area of considerable insecurity for these writers.

One comma usage is worth further comment. The parenthetic comma, the comma which is used in pairs in the same way as brackets might be used, appeared to be a particular feature of the best writing. Confident writers create an effective relationship with their reader, by giving them additional descriptive detail or offering an authorial aside in parenthesis. For example:

> *Mr Brooks, the older farmer, was leaning anxiously against the barn wall.*

Homelessness, as you may have observed, is a problem in our cities.
Britain, on the other hand, is opposed to joining a common European currency .

The use of the apostrophe: No teacher of English will be surprised to read that the possessive apostrophe is frequently used inaccurately, since in many public contexts (from market stalls to academic journals) errors in possessive apostrophe usage have reached epidemic proportions! Even for the best writers, half of all possessive apostrophes are deployed incorrectly.

However, the apostrophe to show omission highlights a further significant difference in the effectiveness of writing for better writers. The best writers are less likely to use an omissive apostrophe than either average or weak writers. One evident reason for this is that the avoidance of contractions aids the achievement of formality of tone in writing. The following two extracts are a response to the same examination question, writing to a headteacher to complain about the decision to discontinue school dinners.

Best writer:
So it is your responsibility to provide for them the one meal a day that can give them some much needed nourishment. If I allow my children money to buy their dinner then I have no doubt that they too will be misled by fatty burgers and chips. I am not saying we should deprive children of this but they should at least have a choice.

Average writer:
That's who I feel sorry for because it isn't cheap doing packed lunches. I strongly believe that you should re-think this through because I think you haven't thought about this at all. I personelly think it's a disgrace and I will be taking action against this.

3   THE USE OF NON-STANDARD ENGLISH

The most significant finding is that, overall, the incidence of non-standard English in writing is low, and is more likely to be a feature of writing from the weakest writers. Looking at the type of non-standard English used, it is clear that in many cases the writers are writing as they speak, reflecting regional or social dialects. For example, using prepositions inappropriately often mirrors conversational style:

I was up a party.
...going straight down Middlesbrough.

A pattern of error which recurs particularly for these weak writers revolves around difficulties with the verb, either subject and verb agreement (e.g. *I were sad*) or confusion between the past tense and the past participle (e.g. *She was sat down*). Other examples of non-standard use in this category include:

Have the lottery made it worse?
Only one in ten thousand get in.
It happens because they was...
Your parents wants you to...

4   CLAUSE STRUCTURE AND WORD CLASS USAGE

Sentences and clauses: The best writing uses a variety of sentence structures and lengths, with some short, simple sentences for effect or emphasis and some longer, complex sentences with effective elaboration. One aspect of this elaboration is that good writers use fewer finite verbs in their sentences because they develop their ideas through the use of adjectives, adverbials and non-finite clauses. By contrast, weak writers are often very dependent upon the finite verb to convey their ideas and they vary the length of their sentences far less. The two examples below illustrate these findings – for ease of reference the finite verbs have been underlined.

Best writer:
Who <u>knows</u> what <u>might</u> lurk around the next corner? The high rise buildings <u>threaten</u> the dark alleys and streets. All <u>is</u> dark and silent. As I <u>watch</u> over the city I <u>see</u> the moonlight catching an office window making it look almost golden. The smells from the rubbish dumped by people shopping and the overloaded bins <u>rises</u> up. The stench <u>is</u> unbelievable like dead bodies left to rot in a cold, damp cellar.

Weak writer:
When I <u>came</u> out she <u>said</u> she <u>was</u> going to run away and never come back. I just <u>said</u> "yes" and <u>carried</u> on to work. At 6.00 when I <u>come</u> home from work I <u>went</u> in her bedroom and some of her clothes <u>had</u> gone. So as I <u>looked</u> in her room I <u>looked</u> she <u>had</u> gone. I <u>sat</u> down and

*phoned the police and they came over and I gave them
a statement and a picture of what she looked like and...*

The best piece has several simple sentences, including one very short sentence for effect (*All is dark and silent*) whereas the piece from the weaker writer has no simple sentences and less variety in sentence length. The finite verbs dominate the portrayal of the narrative with no adjectives and few adverbials. This contrasts with the better piece which has both pre-modification (*dark, cold, damp*) and post-modification (*silent, golden*) and adverbials which help to set the scene for the narrative action (*around the next corner, over the city, in a cold, damp cellar*). Further description is provided by non-finite clauses (*left to rot, catching an office window*).

A further feature of weaker writing is the over-use of co-ordinated clauses, particularly those linked by *and*. Many weak writers connect strings of sentences through co-ordination, giving their writing a somewhat breathless, overwhelming feel:

> *I was very excited when my mum had a baby and then we found out my sister was pregnant and she's had the baby now and it was a boy and it's weight was 9.9 and he is lovely.*

Clearly, this aspect of weaker writing also relates to the insecurity that weaker writers have in ending sentences with a full stop. It may also be true that some average writers use a comma splice where the weakest use *and*.

Word class usage: The decision to look at how individual writers used different word classes was prompted by an interest in how writers choose to convey meaning. As the clause structure section above indicates, the weakest writers often relied quite heavily on the finite verb to drive their writing forward. However, further differences emerged from the analysis of word class usage.

The best writing is also the most lexically dense: in other words, it uses fewer words which have a purely syntactic or grammatical function (such as auxiliary verbs, articles, prepositions, conjunctions) and it makes greater use of the words which carry meaning (nouns, adjectives, adverbs, main verbs). In general, weak writers make little use of adjectives and many of the adverbs used are those which could almost be classified as non-lexical (e.g. *really, just*). Rather like a haiku, where the restriction on the number of syllables permitted forces the writer to choose words carefully, it seems that the good writer is more likely to make every word count than is the weaker.

Another interesting finding to emerge is that the most accomplished writers make greater use of the abstract noun, especially in narrative writing. This is probably because good writers sometimes use an abstract noun where less capable writers might have chosen to use an adjective. For example,

> *The peace moved me* (rather than *It was peaceful*)
> *Anger flushed her face* (rather than *She was angry*)

In other circumstances, more liberal use of abstract nouns reflect a higher degree of abstraction and distance in the narrative voice:

> *Nobody minds the noise. It is all part of the atmosphere. A shaft of light momentarily fills the room as the doors open to let a newcomer enter. Some turn around to see the source of the disturbance while others just blink in the unnatural light. Legs lie sprawled over seats or cramped between the aisles. The tawdry music invades the stillness and I feel somehow violated of my peace.*

5   PARAGRAPHING

Although the project identified the predictable pattern that weaker writers rarely use paragraphs while the best writers invariably do, some of the most interesting findings related to the way in which paragraphs are linked. Average writers sometimes have limited access to a repertoire of similar ways of opening paragraphs and so some of their paragraph links are repetitive (*I think...I think...I think*). In contrast, the best writers are more able to play with subtle variations of vocabulary, thus avoiding the repetition:

> *I know; I wish; I hope;*
> *I am aware; I can remember; I am sure;*

Moreover, the best writers are more likely to structure each paragraph around a clearly identifiable topic, whereas for an average writer the paragraph structuring is sometimes less assured.

In narrative writing, time adverbials are commonly used at all grades to link paragraphs, but the exact nature of those time adverbials varies. The very small number of weak writers who use paragraphs rely more on the adverb (*today; then; still, now*) whereas more confident writers use adverbials or a main clause specifying time. The best writers are able to manage the time setting more subtly and to use less common adverbs. The table below shows some of these differences.

Best Writer	*The night lives*
	The time had come
	Eventually
	Currently
	As the day progressed
Average Writer	*It was seven fourteen p.m*
	It was 12.30
	It was a Saturday
	It was time for
	At night
Weak Writer	*Today*
	Then
	Still
	Now
	After

Overall, writers make greater use of time adverbials than place adverbials, suggesting that in narrative, most writers think primarily about action and events rather than about setting and location. Only for the best writers does the number of place adverbials used parallel the number of time adverbials. Where a place adverbial is positioned at the start of the sentence, it appears to have more impact because the setting is foregrounded:

Towards the left...
Between the sand and...
In a slightly quieter corner...

In non-narrative writing, differences in the way paragraphs signal contrasts or sequences of ideas are evident. Weaker writers tend to order ideas through repetitive structures (e.g. *the second thing; the third thing; the last thing;* or *the first point, the second point*) whereas able writers indicate more variety (*firstly, finally*). Likewise, in writing which requires paragraphs to contrast ideas, weaker writers have a very limited repertoire, using *but* frequently, and occasionally using *anyway* or *at least*. The best writers are the only ones to use *however* and other linking structures found only in the best writing include *yet, admittedly* and *even so*.

6   TEXTUAL ORGANISATION

There are clear differences in the way writers of different abilities organise text. Overall, writers are more confident with opening writing appropriately and with establishing a reader-writer relationship than with closure or maintaining cohesion and coherence. Successful openings use description effectively to set a context and are able to establish the genre of the piece. The following comments on writing openings gives some indication of the range of strengths and weaknesses in this area:

- *concise evocation of darkness; worlds of light and shadow effectively introduced; establishes secret world;*
- *indicates theme, but weak in genre; signals theme effectively; opts for letter form but genre is eye-witness report; eye-witness genre not well signalled;*
- *no clues to... setting; little detail re character or context; setting and time-frame weak.*

One difficulty with cohesion and coherence for all writers tends to revolve around unclear or poorly managed use of pronouns or names:

- *the central "I" character is rather fragmented; needs to use names more* (A grade);
- *some confusion over we and* our; *some confusion over* our *and* they (A grade);
- *moves between you and I haphazardly; you becomes confusing;* (C grade);
- *use of pronouns in an uncontrolled way; pronoun* you *sometimes confusing* (C grade);
- *weak use of pronouns; who took him down?; shift to we not explained* (F grade);
- they *used in first sentence without previous reference;* you *used without indication or audience; pronouns not well used* (F grade).

Although the predictable pattern of good writers being more competent in all aspects of textual organisation is apparent, interesting teaching implications emerge from the analysis. For example, the best and average writers have the same pattern of strengths, namely that the reader-writer relationship and openings are more effective than cohesion and coherence or closure. However, the best writers have an additional strength in their capacity to establish a good relationship with the reader and to open texts appropriately. However, although they are markedly better than average writers in maintaining cohesion and coherence, and in ending texts effectively, these two aspects of their writing are typically the least successful. Endings are often perfunctory, rather than carefully crafted or shaped, and comments on the endings written even by the best writers include:

- *not so much a resolution as a new development;*
- *simply an echo of the start - hasn't gone anywhere;*
- *misses the opportunity to round off the report.*

Although these are examination scripts and written under controlled conditions, teaching the most able writers more about the ways in which cohesion is created in a text and looking explicitly at how texts can be closed effectively would clearly meet these writers' needs.

THE PATTERN OF PERFORMANCE IN TEXTUAL ORGANISATION		
Best writers	**Average**	**Weakest**
Reader-writer relationship Openings ↓ Cohesion/coherence Closure	Reader-writer relationship Openings Cohesion/coherence Closure	Openings Endings ↓ Reader-writer relationship Cohesion / coherence

By contrast, average writers present a less clear pattern of strengths and weaknesses, with all four aspects of textual organisation being rated as reasonably successful. For the weakest writers, the pattern of confidence changed, with openings and endings being their most successful features. Textual organisation generally is very weak in their writing overall but they also appear to have a particularly poor understanding of the reader-writer relationship and of how to keep a text cohesive and coherent.

RELATED ISSUES

GENDER DIFFERENCES IN WRITING

The project raised some interesting questions about writing and gender, particularly in the light of current concerns about boys' underachievement in English. The sample was not fully gender-balanced because there was a preponderance of boys at grade F so, in order to compare boys' and girls' writing, the F grade sample was discounted and only A and C grade compared. The differences which emerged were often very small, too small to make reliable claims about patterns of difference but the results were surprising because the trend was consistent in pointing to a superior performance by boys, other than in the accurate use of speech marks. The main findings were that boys:

- used more sophisticated vocabulary than girls;
- made more accurate and frequent use of the comma than girls;
- made more use of the parenthetic comma;
- handled clauses better than girls;
- were stronger in all aspects of textual organisation than girls.

Meanwhile, girls used more dialogue than boys and were more accurate in their use of speech marks. These results cry out for further investigation. Is this just a quirk of the statistics or are boys actually better at crafting and shaping their writing? If so, why do they not get higher grades? Is it possible that teachers and markers are alienated by what boys write about, or their presentation and pay less attention to how well they have written?

INTERRELATIONSHIPS IN LANGUAGE FEATURES

One of the most fascinating aspects of the Technical Accuracy Project was the way in which various linguistic features inter-related with each other. In particular, many of the sentence level linguistic features had an effect upon the success of the whole text. This underlines that it is difficult to separate mechanistically the 'surface features' of writing from the content, as is often the case. The way a text is written is intrinsically related to how successfully it communicates – what is written is affected by how it is written. Some examples of such inter-relationships include the following.

The use of the full stop and clause/sentence structure

Writers who did not use full stops at all or used comma splices needed to look more closely at their clause and sentence structure, which was often poorly handled. Additionally, writers who tended to use excessive co-ordination needed a clearer grasp of how sentence demarcation or internal sentence punctuation could separate clauses and sentences more effectively.

Clause structure and textual cohesion

One cause of a loss of cohesion was often poor handling of clauses, particularly where subordinators were used awkwardly or ambiguously and where the sequencing of tenses broke down.

Excessive co-ordination and the reader-writer relationship

The use of excessive co-ordination made it difficult for the reader to engage with the text, or established an inappropriately fast pace, thus creating a negative influence on the reader-writer relationship. In addition, the presence of excessive co-ordination often meant the absence of detail and description to meet the needs of a reader.

Parenthetic commas and the reader-writer relationship

The use of parenthetical commas frequently helped to establish a positive reader-writer relationship. The text inside parenthetic commas in narrative often provided additional detail or qualification for the reader, whilst in non-narrative, it was often in the form of an aside or a direct address to the reader.

Omissive apostrophe and the establishment of formality in the reader-writer relationship

Writers who used a high frequency of omissive apostrophes in a formal text often undermined their attempt at formality of tone through their use of many contractions. By contrast, writers who chose to use uncontracted forms established a more formal tone.

This chart overleaf summarises the findings of the Technical Accuracy Project in relation to GCSE grades.

CHARACTERISTICS OF WRITING AT DIFFERENT	
Grade	**A**
PUNCTUATION	♦ accurate; ♦ includes variety of devices; ♦ commas used to support meaning; ♦ use of commas parenthetically; ♦ omissive apostrophe correct.
CLAUSE STRUCTURE	♦ variety in sentences: simple and multiple; ♦ sentences expanded by adverbials/non-finite clauses; ♦ considerably more subordination than co-ordination; ♦ effective use of sub. and co-ordination; ♦ varied subordinating/co-ordinating conjunctions.
WORD CLASS	♦ greater use of abstract nouns; ♦ greater lexical density; ♦ lower number of finite verbs.

SPELLING	♦ mean accuracy: 99%
	♦ errors with:-
	    - separating compound words into two words;
	    - doubling consonants;
	    - unstressed vowels.

PARAGRAPHING	♦ paragraphing nearly always present and used accurately; ♦ a greater variety of paragraph linkage using conjuncts to compare and contrast.
TEXTUAL ORGANISATION	♦ establishes good relationship with reader; ♦ successful openings; ♦ less successful closure and cohesion/coherence.

GCSE GRADES (BORDERLINE)

C	F
<ul><li>generally accurate;</li><li>comma splicing evident;</li><li>commas used to demarcate some clauses and in lists, but rarely parenthetically;</li><li>omissive apostrophe correct; greater use of contractions;</li><li>errors in possessive apostrophe.</li></ul>	<ul><li>generally accurate use of capital letter;</li><li>widespread omission of punctuation, especially the full stop;</li><li>sparse use of commas;</li><li>errors in both omissive and possessive apostrophes.</li></ul>
<ul><li>less variety in sentence structure;</li><li>more long sentences, fewer simple sentences;</li><li>more subordination than co-ordination;</li><li>some weaknesses in handling clause structure, especially co-ordination;</li><li>conjunctions used are less varied.</li></ul>	<ul><li>less variety in structure; some repetitive structures;</li><li>almost equal use of co-ordination and subordination; problems with strings of clauses linked by 'and';</li><li>weaknesses in handling clauses.</li></ul>
<ul><li>higher number of finite verbs;</li><li>some use of abstract nouns;</li><li>reliance on adjectives and adverbs for detail.</li></ul>	<ul><li>little use of abstract nouns;</li><li>lower lexical density;</li><li>highest number of finite verbs;</li><li>more reliance on adverbs, but low use of adjectives.</li></ul>
<ul><li>mean accuracy: 97%</li><li>errors with:-<ul><li>- separating compound words;</li><li>- omission;</li><li>- homophones;</li><li>- unstressed vowels.</li></ul></li></ul>	<ul><li>mean accuracy: 94%</li><li>many errors difficult to categorise;</li><li>letters and phonemes omitted;</li><li>words often phonetically plausible;</li><li>word division less significant than for A & C.</li></ul>
<ul><li>paragraphing usually present and handled appropriately in 50% of cases where it is used;</li><li>less variety of linkage than at A.</li></ul>	<ul><li>paragraphing as likely to be omitted as used;</li><li>limited number of paragraphs means limited range of paragraph links, particularly in non-narrative.</li></ul>
<ul><li>generally successful relationship with reader and openings(though less strong than A grade);</li><li>less successful closure;</li><li>less successful cohesion/coherence.</li></ul>	<ul><li>some success in openings and closure but very little success in establishing relationship with reader;</li><li>lack of cohesion.</li></ul>

5 KEY FACTORS IN WRITING SUCCESS

In addition to the analysis of pupils' writing in GCSE English examinations, QCA also commissioned the evaluation agency for the 1999 National Curriculum English tests to undertake a parallel analysis. The same coding frames were used, this time to investigate writing across the key stages, from Key Stage 1 to Key Stage 3. More detailed findings of this evaluation can be found in the report booklets sent to schools (*Standards at Key Stage 3 English: Report on the 1999 national curriculum assessments for 14 year olds* and the parallel documents for Key Stages 1 and 2). It is worth noting that, for the first time, this analysis allowed substantive and detailed comparisons of pupils' writing to be made across key stages.

Perhaps the most significant finding is that at every stage the profile of best writing mirrors the overall patterns identified in the Technical Accuracy Project. It is not surprising that accuracy is greater in better writers as that confirms what we would expect – at age 7, 11 and 14 the best writers are more accurate in spelling, punctuation and paragraphing than their less accomplished peers. But, what is more interesting is that the pattern of linguistic features which characterises an A grade GCSE text is broadly similar to the pattern revealed by Level 7 writers at Key Stage 3, by level 5 writers at Key Stage 2 and, to a lesser extent, by level 3 writers at Key Stage 1. In other words, the tendency is for the best writers at each key stage to use fewer finite verbs, to move away from use of co-ordination towards the use of subordination, to manage the reader-writer relationship more effectively, and so on. This suggests that development in writing within a key stage and across key stages follows a similar pattern and that development is not strongly age-related but is, instead, ability-related.

This is not to say, of course, that a Key Stage 1 level 3 piece of writing is the same as an A grade GCSE script. The best writers at GCSE are more accurate and more accomplished than their younger peers. But what it does imply is that the best writers move towards greater accuracy and sophistication through the same routes, from Key Stage 1 right through to GCSE.

However, the cross-key stage analysis also provides some indications of which aspects of writing might be more relevant at a given key stage. If, instead of looking separately at the differences between weak writers and good writers at each key stage, the average profile of a writer is taken, some interesting patterns emerge. The principal findings can be linked to aspects of clause and word class usage, paragraphing, punctuation and textual organisation:

Where clause use is concerned, there is significantly more co-ordination than subordination at Key Stage 1, marginally more co-ordination than subordination at Key Stage 2, and more subordination than co-ordination at Key Stage 3. Sentences become longer and use more clauses – the biggest difference is between Key Stage 2 and Key Stage 3. Then, at GCSE level, there is more sentence variety including short and long, and simple and multiple sentences.

Writers at Key Stage 3 are better at linking paragraphs and organising text; they use more conjuncts, more adverbials, and more structural patterning. Where punctuation is concerned, although accurate use of full stops and capitalisation improves with key stage, there is not much development in accuracy after Key Stage 2 (Key Stage 2 - 71%; Key Stage 3 - 74%; KS4 -72%).

However, writers at Key Stage 2 are more accurate in their use of the possessive apostrophe and speech marks; and make greater use of colons and semi-colons than happens at Key Stage 3. The overall impression is that punctuation declines at key stages 3 and 4, with less accuracy overall and less use of devices such as commas and speech marks, presumably as purposes for writing and communicative intentions become more complex. Textual organisation improves with key stage and, at every stage, openings are better than endings. There is a significant improvement in textual organisation between levels 4 and 5 at Key Stage 2.

For teachers of secondary English, these findings should sound a powerful alarm bell. What is happening to punctuation at key stages 3 and 4? Rather than improving as they get older, secondary writers appear to be deteriorating in their use of punctuation. This is not simply in terms of accuracy, but also in terms of frequency of usage. It was noticeable in the GCSE analysis that many of the weakest writers had abandoned punctuation altogether, and that many average writers demarcated sentences with comma splices; even in the best writing there were relatively few semi-colons and colons.

As a profession, teachers have always been more confident about what constitutes development in reading whereas our descriptions of development in writing tend to have been confined to improvement in accuracy levels and improvement in appropriacy for audience and purpose. To take one illustration of this, the Initial Teacher Training curriculum for secondary English teachers describes for trainee teachers what progression looks like in oracy, reading and writing (*Circular 4/98, DfEE 1998*). The contrast between the specificity of the oracy and reading progression criteria and the vagueness of the writing criteria is stark.

Speaking and Listening:

from *being able to speak to different audiences with some adaptation* **to** *sustained adaptation of speech to the needs and interests of different audiences, including more formal speech when appropriate;*
from *identifying the key points of what is heard and how these are presented* **to** *a discriminating appreciation of what has been heard, attending to the main messages and their impact, and the detail and techniques used;*
from *contributing and responding in discussion, taking on a number of roles,* **to** *making a substantial contribution to the effectiveness of group discussion, including through taking a leading role;*
from *exploring a range of dramatic forms and conventions to represent ideas and issues* **to** *adapting and using these to generate their own dramatic representations of character and action.*

Reading:

from *reading and responding to straightforward and familiar texts* **to** *an appreciation of varied and challenging texts;*
from *inference and deduction of simple meanings* **to** *grasping other layers of meaning and an appreciation of writers' techniques in realising them;*
from *use of specific evidence from texts to support views* **to** *marshalling reasons and evidence for a sustained critical analysis;*
from *finding and using accessible information* **to** *researching, extracting and synthesising information independently.*

Writing:

from *writing in simple, familiar formats for different purposes*
to *independent composition of texts tailored to their audience and purpose;*
from *accurate and consistent use of the conventions of grammar, spelling and punctuation in straightforward contexts* **to** *accurate use of them in more complex texts.*

In contrast, the outcomes of both the Technical Accuracy Project and of the evaluation of national tests in English do make it possible to identify patterns of progression and development which can inform our teaching. It enables teachers to be more precise about how writing improves and to direct teaching more explicitly to those areas which will help writing to develop. The table below summarises the principal progression criteria in terms of linguistic competence.

PROGRESSION CRITERIA IN PUPIL WRITING

from		to	
	◆ heavy use of finite verbs		◆ decreased use of finite verbs
	◆ little use of adjectives and adverbs		◆ greater use of adjectives and adverbs
	◆ little use of abstract nouns		◆ greater use of abstract nouns
	◆ short sentences		◆ long and short sentences
	◆ similar sentence types		◆ variety in sentence types
	◆ greater use of co-ordination		◆ greater use of subordination
	◆ no paragraphs		◆ paragraph use
	◆ poor paragraph links		◆ accomplished paragraph links
	◆ opening texts effectively		◆ ending texts effectively
	◆ writing for self		◆ writing for a reader

These criteria are central to the development of better writing but, as teachers will note, have not been the focus of teaching and learning in the past. It may well be the case that what is required at Key Stage 3 and Key Stage 4 is not a new pedagogy but a reformed writing curriculum.

6   CLASSROOM PRACTICE 2

Analysing writing features below the levels of paragraph and textual organisation

Looking at some actual examples of children's writing can help to illustrate effectively how development in writing can be seen across differing levels of ability and how more precise attention to the linguistic characteristics of a piece of writing can enable more focused responses to the work.

Firstly, let us consider extracts of writing from GCSE grades A, C and F in terms of their linguistic features below the levels of paragraph and textual organisation. The extracts are exactly one hundred words in length. In particular, consider the clause and sentence characteristics of each piece. For ease of identification, the finite verbs have been underlined, subordinate clauses have been marked by square brackets and co-ordinating conjunctions marked in bold print.

A cursory skim-read of the three pieces will quickly reveal the three differing proficiencies in writing, but precisely how do they differ, and how can an analysis of such a small snippet of a child's writing provide any useful illumination?

GCSE A GRADE:

There was the place [that we stopped being children] **and** turned into animals **or** fishermen or whatever the game allowed us to be. One day our tree was a boat. Another it was a house. The gentle flowing river was a swamp infested with wild crocodiles (symbolised by little fish or small twigs floating down stream) or a crashing rapid endangering all of our lives. Here was the place [we exercised our minds], [where we let our imagination run freely.] [When we were in our own little world] it was amazing [what we would make of an innocuous little ...]

GCSE C GRADE:

It <u>was</u> very quiet **and** I <u>was</u> watching television [when the smell <u>hit</u> me.] My worst fears had come true. I <u>had</u> to change his dirty nappy **and** I <u>wasn't</u> looking forward to it. (My cousin <u>had</u> briefed me generally on how to change one, quickly [before she <u>went</u>] **but** that <u>was</u> no use.)

I <u>had</u> put it on back to front, upside down **and** finally after thirty minutes of Corrie wriggling and slapping me in the face I <u>had</u> succeeded. Well it <u>looked</u> right anyway. I <u>gave</u> him some supper **and** [as the night <u>passed</u> by] he <u>became</u> restless...

GCSE F GRADE:

we <u>started</u> to throw bricks in the canal [where he <u>had</u> gone in] **and** he still never <u>came</u> back. so I **and** 2 other chaps <u>went</u> for help **and** <u>left</u> [where he <u>feel</u> in]. We <u>went</u> to the factory just up the canal **and** they <u>helped</u> us. 2 workmen <u>jumped</u> in the canal looking for him. they <u>got</u> him **but** he <u>wasn't</u> breathing **so** we <u>called</u> an ambulance. they <u>took</u> him to the hospital **and** they <u>couldn't</u> get him to breathe. the doctor <u>asked</u> [how long he <u>had</u> been under the water for] **and** I <u>said</u> only for a ...

A brief numerical analysis reveals the following about the use of finite verbs and co-ordinated and subordinate clauses.

Grade	No of sentences	Finite verbs	co-ordinated clauses	subordinate clauses
A	5	13	2	5
C	6	15	5	3
F	6	17	7	3

Now, let us consider each extract in turn. Firstly, the A grade piece evokes a strong sense of emotional involvement, achieved through the use of emotive vocabulary which conveys to the reader the scope of the children's imaginative play (*infested; crashing; endangering; amazing; innocuous*). Adjectival premodification creates further pictorial detail (*gentle flowing; little, small*).

The sentence structure is varied, with the effective use of two short, simple sentences in sequence but counterpointing each other (*One day our tree was a boat. Another it was a house.*). The remaining simple sentence is long and elaborated, depicting the gentle flowing river in its different imaginary manifestations. It makes use of several non-finite clauses (*infested...; symbolised .. floating downstream; endangering...*) and adverbials (*with wild crocodiles; by little fish*) which contribute descriptive and emotional detail. The demonstrative pronouns which open the first and fourth sentence balance each other and move the viewpoint of the reader from a distant *There* to a more present *Here*. The final sentence of the extract fronts the subordinate clause, reversing a more standard main clause–subordinate clause order, and thus giving additional emphasis *to our own imaginary world*.

The co-ordination in the first sentences establishes the narrative action of the piece, telling the reader what the children did in their imaginary world. But, it is the subordination which allows the writer to reflect upon the significance of the narrative action and to record that it was in this special place *that we stopped being children, where we let our imagination run freely and exercised our minds*.

The pattern of this child's writing fits perfectly the profile of an A grade writer. Finite verbs are used sparingly, with sentences expanded by non-finite clauses, adjectives and adverbials. There is a variety in sentence length and type, with both short and long sentences, and simple and multiple sentences. Co-ordination is restricted in use, whilst subordination is used more widely. Overall, the writing is less heavily claused than either the C or F grade pieces, because of the use of some simple sentences.

Now, let us look more closely at the C grade piece. This piece uses more finite verbs than the A grade extract (fifteen compared with thirteen in the A grade piece) but there is some elaboration within the sentence. Adjectives are deployed to provide additional detail, though these are relatively commonplace adjectives which frequently collocate with the following noun (*worst fears; dirty nappy*). The non-finite clause *wriggling and slapping me in the face* creates further narrative detail with humorous overtones, a humour intensified by splitting *finally* from the rest of its clause (*I had succeeded*) in order to describe the difficulty experienced. Although the resulting sentence is slightly awkward, there is a sense in this sentence of a writer trying to achieve a deliberate effect through crafting what is said, from the initial images of the failed attempts (*upside down, back-to-front*) through to hard-won success.

The writer uses two simple sentences, both of which emphasise the protagonist's viewpoint and take the reader out of the narrative action into a comment upon it. The first, (*My worst fears had come true*) draws our attention to the baby-sitter's understandable feelings about nappy-changing, whilst the second (*Well it looked alright anyway*) is a wry modification of the reference to success in the previous sentence. In both these examples, the short simple sentences contribute to the reader-writer relationship by inviting readers to see the narrative events from the protagonist's perspective.

The sentences tend to repeat the subject-verb-object pattern, with no inversions or fronted subordinate clauses: this is underlined by the repetition of *I* or *My* at the start of several sentences. There is greater use of co-ordination than subordination, though the co-ordination does contribute partially to the effectiveness of the narrative recount. The subordination is simple, largely providing additional time-related narrative detail.

Overall, this piece is typical of many GCSE grade C pieces. It exemplifies a writer who is able to elaborate within the sentence with some success and who is using adjectives, non-finite clauses and adverbials to provide this elaboration. The vocabulary or images chosen may not be highly imaginative but they do, nonetheless, help the reader to identify with the narrative events. There is some variety in sentence types, with two short, simple sentences but the sentence structure tends towards repetitiveness and co-ordination is used more extensively than subordination.

Finally, let us look at the GCSE grade F piece and the patterns it presents. Here, the use of finite verbs is more or less the only means of conveying narrative action and the higher frequency (seventeen, compared with fifteen and thirteen at C and A grades) creates a noticeably faster pace. However, this pace is at the expense of the reader's needs and there is little attention to descriptive detail or to authorial comment. There are no adjectives used and elaboration within the sentence relies largely upon place adverbials (*in the canal; to the hospital*). These place adverbials provide the only descriptions of setting for the narrative events and in themselves are fairly rudimentary, creating a narrative which could have occurred in any canal near to any factory. The generalised nature of the account is further emphasised by the use of pronouns, with no named persons occurring in this extract at all.

The sentences do not vary substantially in length, or structure, and most are composed of two or more co-ordinated clauses. The one simple sentence (*2 workmen jumped in the canal looking for him*) is not used for any particular effect. The co-ordination is over-used, contributing to the breathless pace of the piece and preventing any distancing from the action to consider its consequences or emotional reactions of the participants.

This writing is typical of many F grade pieces. It relies heavily on finite verbs to deliver the narrative account and offers the reader little in the way of descriptive or reflective detail. Co-ordination is used too much, with a correspondingly limited use of subordination. There is little variety in sentence length or structure and the writing is more heavily claused than either A or C grade pieces.

7 CLASSROOM PRACTICE 3

Analysing features of writing at text level

Considering writing as a whole text is the most usual way of responding to children's writing: as English teachers we are all very familiar with reading work to evaluate how successful it is in being appropriate for its intended audience, its purpose and its form. However, looking more closely at a piece in terms of its textual organisation can provide surprisingly rich information about *how* a writer is managing audience, purpose and form.

To explore this in more detail let us look at two pieces of examination writing from a GCSE grade A candidate. The first is a non-narrative piece, written to fulfil the requirements of *writing to argue, persuade and instruct*, and the second, a narrative piece written to fulfil the requirements of *writing to inform, explain and describe*.

This first piece was written in response to stimulus material concerning the effects of television on children: candidates were invited to write a leaflet persuading parents of the dangers to their children of too much television-watching.

The task was:

Write an article for a magazine aimed at parents. Argue the case for or against children being allowed to have a television in their bedrooms to watch whatever they like, whenever they like.

Below is the candidate's response:

TV OR NOT TV?

Have you ever considired what television is doing to your child? Do you know what dangers lie in your child being able to watch what they want, when they want?

Frankly, most parents do not. In millions of houses across the world children have televisions in their bedrooms which they can watch when they want. This massive independence can be of benefit or hindrance to the childs progress both socially and educationally.

However, many peoples argument for children owning a TV is the opposite; if children are allowed a TV in their rooms then they will watch educational programmes when, say, the rest of the family may be watching a film. Is this what you think? Well, unsurprisingly, this is the opinion shared by many thousands of parents in the UK. But this is rarely the case: don't fall into the same trap.

Evidence collected shows that parents underestimate the sheer breadth of programmes avalible on TV today. A TV in a childs room can allow them to watch 'adult' movies late at night, or can distract them from revision. Surely you don't want this to happen to your child?

However, whatever movies are shown, television, as you will know, can be educational, but the reality is that much of it is pure fiction and is of harm to your child. Reading is of much more benefit than TV, and so should be encouraged. Independent research has proven that TV watching raises stress levels and decreases your child's concentration span, whilst reading promotes concentration and reduces stress. However, many adults ignore such research, and pass it off as rubbish. You assume that a TV will give your child a sense of responsibility; but can you afford to be so foolish?

As you read this, research is taking place into a link between TV watching and attention deficit disorder. Giving your child a TV in their room will not only dent their education, but will also effect their health. Giving your child a television in their room may increase their freedom, but it _will_ damage their health and education. At the end of the day the decision is up to you; but do you want to disadvantage your child's hope of success in life?

The opening uses the device of rhetorical questions to capture the reader's attention and to cut straight to the heart of the issue. There is no preamble and the use of the second person is a direct address to the reader, even a challenge (Do you know...?). The use of you and your reminds the reader of his or her parental responsibilities and prevents the reader from considering the arguments to be expressed as relevant only to others. Subordination is used skilfully by paralleling 'what they want, when they want' to emphasise the complete freedom some children are given over their television viewing.

The paragraphs are linked in a variety of ways. The second paragraph opens with an answer to the rhetorical questions of the first paragraph: it contrasts the assumed responsible duty of care provided by the parent readers of the opening with the foolish carelessness of most parents. The short, simple sentence and the blunt adverb *frankly* signal the argument which follows. Further paragraphs contrast or challenge ideas previously introduced (e.g. paragraph 3), or develop an argument previously introduced (e.g. paragraphs 4 and 5). The conjunct, *however*, is used twice as a paragraph opening to indicate contrast or development.

Closure is achieved with some success. The first sentence of the final paragraph summarises the argument of the whole piece, reiterating assertively that televisions in bedrooms will damage their health and education. The sentence counterpoints the modals *may* and *will* cleverly, suggesting that a possible benefit on one hand is outweighed by a certain disadvantage on the other. The reference to freedom echoes the opening reference to allowing children to watch what they want, when they want. The final sentence mirrors the rhetorical questions of the opening and shifts again from the third person facts of the previous sentence, to the second person address, handing the responsibility for decision-making to the reader. The lexis is emotive and judgmental (*damage*, *disadvantage*, *hope*, *success*) implying that there is only one possible answer to the question posed. Arguably, however, the final sentence, particularly the allusion to 'hope of success in life' is neither as powerful nor as subtle as the previous sentence.

As with many A grade pieces, the reader-writer relationship is particularly well-managed in this piece. The opening device of rhetorical questions is repeated at several points throughout the piece as a constant reminder to readers that the argument is addressing them personally, reinforced by the use of the second person in all the rhetorical questions. The third person voice establishes the argument against television in children's bedrooms and describes the research which lends weight to this argument. Additionally, the third person voice creates a sense of objectivity and distance which contrasts with the directness of the 'you' address: the writing is successfully persuasive because it manipulates the more emotive, personalised challenges of the second person with the more factual, academic arguments of the third person. The imperative is used to alert parents to potential dangers - *don't fall into the same trap* - and again attempts to place 'the reader' in an advantaged position compared to 'other parents'. Parenthetic asides (*as you will know, as you read this*) interrupt the factual research evidence to acknowledge the reader's presence, and to bridge the gap between a reader's personal experience and the more abstract findings of academic research. Finally, the writer considered the visual layout of the text by indicating a graphics box in the script which would support the anti-television argument by presenting comparative data on concentration spans. The 'colourful' graphics would help the reader locate key information and reinforce the key argument.

Cohesion and coherence are generally sustained throughout. The present tense is consistently and appropriately used, and the balance of nouns and pronouns achieves coherence in meaning (although there is a repeated tendency to use a singular noun followed by a plural pronoun – e.g. *child, their*). The theme of the merits or otherwise of television in bedrooms is sustained throughout, as is the stand taken by the writer against bedroom televisions. Repetition of *you* and *your child* supports the cohesion as do verbal echoes from one paragraph to another (*movies: movies* – paragraphs 4 and 5; *health: health* – paragraphs 7 and 8). The lexical harmony is maintained well with emotive vocabulary:

> *benefit, hindrance, dangers, distract, damage, disadvantage, hope, success;*

and the sustained vocabulary of academic research;

> *evidence, research, stress levels, concentration spans, attention deficit disorder, health, socially, educationally.*

One small slip in coherence is evident in the opening of the third paragraph which refers slightly ambiguously to *the opposite* of an idea mentioned in the previous paragraph. Although it becomes clear that it is the notion of hindrance which is intended, initially the reader is uncertain whether it is the benefit or the hindrance of television viewing which is being referred to.

This detailed analysis of the way this writer has shaped the text illuminates how the success of the piece has been achieved. Importantly, however, it also illuminates how this writer might be encouraged to develop and is a reminder that considering writing in terms of its linguistic features is not simply about 'remedial' work for weaker writers but has much to offer writers of all abilities. So this writer might be advised to consider working on the use of:

- conjuncts other than 'however', which could be used to link paragraphs or signal contrasts, to summarise or to refocus;
- rhetorical questions and whether they have been slightly over-used in this piece;
- cohesion and how to improve it by correcting the singular subject/plural pronoun disagreements;
- different strategies and devices used to end persuasive pieces.

In the second piece, candidates were invited to write a narrative about a journey under the broad headings of inform, explain, describe. Before going on to read the commentary, you may wish to think about the writing features that you would note in this piece. The task was:

Journeys can be exciting, boring or a mixture of both. Describe a journey you have made, so that the reader can imagine it clearly.

Below is the candidate's response:

A Journey

It was three o'clock on a cold, wet Saturday as our car swept out of the drive with me inside. The wind could be heard howling through the trees, over the noise of the engine. The sodium street-lighting threw eerie shadows over the village square as we sped through. Tired and bored at the prospect of a long journey, I thought of going to France to relax and revise. Sitting in the back-left seat of the car, I imagined what I would be doing in France on the next day, and the next week.

My attention was soon drawn away from my imagination as we passed onto the motorway. I could hear the faint, yet distinctive, siren of a police car behind us and became suddenly alert: was the motorway blocked; would we not get to France? I was soon relaxed, though, as it hurtled past us, its blue lights causing the sleeping faces of my mother and brother to be lit in a morbid, cold blue. As time went on, and dad turned Radio 4, World Service, on, I drifted slowly off to sleep, first waking every minute or so and pretending to have been awake, and then into a long slumber.

I woke to sunlight knifing the clean blue sky, and the sound of seagulls piercing the air...

... [further paragraphs describing the journey]

The hotel loomed out of the horizon, eclipsing the sharp rays of the sun. We pulled into the car park; decorated with flower beds and fountains, it was like no car park I had ever seen. The engine stopped, and the handbrake was pulled on. I stepped out of the car, allowing my muscles to streatch for the first time in quite a while, with relief that the journey was over. The cold north wind stabbed at my face, as I noticed storm clouds forming on the horizon.

The opening quickly establishes a time frame (*three o'clock*) and a setting (*the drive*) and includes additional information about the weather which conveys a mood for the events which follow. The *cold, wet* weather and the *howling* wind make an inauspicious start to a journey which the *tired and bored* protagonist is not looking forward to, although it is made evident that the visit to France itself should be a pleasurable opportunity for relaxation and revision. Thus a narrative problem is set: how will the traveller cope with a tedious journey?

Paragraph links make considerable use of the device of a topic sentence, which introduces a new development in the narrative. For example, the second paragraph moves the setting on to the motorway and the 'red herring' appearance of a police car, while the third paragraph shifts the time frame from night to daytime. A strong feature of the way paragraphs are linked in this piece is the use of verbal echoes to reinforce connections between paragraphs. The final sentence of the first paragraph and the first sentence of the second paragraph both mention the theme of imagination, whilst the second and third paragraphs are linked by the verbal contrast of *slumber* and *woke*.

The closure is well crafted with many references back to the opening. A contrast is established between the night-time setting of the opening and daytime setting of the end. The narrative problem has moved to its resolution with the completion of the journey, emphasised by the mechanical actions of stopping the car and by the reflective comment, noting relief that *the journey was over*. A deft touch is the introduction of slight ambiguity in the final sentence, with its reference to imminent bad weather echoing the stormy weather of the start, and casting a possible shadow over the anticipated pleasure of the stay. The last sentence also avoids the more simplistic closure of ending the piece with the end of the journey, and leaves the reader with a new problem to consider.

In this narrative, the reader-writer relationship is supported largely through the provision of detail which allows the reader to picture the scene. Throughout, the writer elaborates upon the narrative action to evoke pictorial detail, from the *sodium street-lighting* of home to the sun and seagulls of France; and from the faces of the passengers turned a *morbid, cold blue* by the police lights to the French hotel *looming* ahead *eclipsing* the sunlight. Adverbials provide details of both place and time:

> *on a cold, wet Saturday; out of the horizon; over the village square; for the first time...*

whilst non-finite clauses offer further elaboration:

> *piercing the air; sitting in the back-left seat; allowing my muscles to stretch...*

In addition, the narrative is written from a clear viewpoint which is sustained throughout. The reader is invited to see the journey from the protagonist's viewpoint. Early on we learn his seating position in the car. We are allowed to share his feelings when he hears the police car, *alert* and then *relaxed*; we watch, with the protagonist, the effects of the blue lights on his mother and brother's faces. We are also privy to his pretence to be awake as he drifts off to sleep and to his surprise at the lavishly decorated car park in France. Overall, the reader shares the movement through the narrative from anticipated boredom to eventual relief.

Cohesion and coherence are both sustained throughout. The first person voice and past tense are consistent, maintaining both cohesion and sustaining the genre. The theme is coherently developed and resolved, and changes in setting (England to France) and time (night to day) are carefully managed. The narrative adopts a straightforward chronology framed by the time and place shifts of the journey. The vocabulary of the piece is appropriate to the form and there is lexical harmony through the writing. This is evident in the cluster of words associated with feelings (*tired, bored, alert, relaxed, relief*) and the vocabulary of the weather with its over-arching pattern of hostile weather (*cold, wet; north wind; howling; storm clouds*) contrasting with the emergence of bright sunlight. There is also an underlying lexical pattern of threat, largely created by the hostile weather (*knifing; sharp, stabbed*), but also apparent in the *eerie shadows* of the street lights, the *morbid blue faces* in the car and the *looming* hotel *eclipsing* the light.

What, then, might this successful writer consider in order to develop further competence in writing skills? There are no substantial weaknesses but the following points might merit further attention:

- how to use alternative chronologies for personal narratives, rather than the straightforward recount of an event from beginning to end;
- how to improve description by avoiding the obvious, almost cliched, descriptions perhaps by building on the originality of the image of the police lights turning faces a *morbid, cold blue* and avoiding the commonplace images like the *howling* wind which *stabs*.

Looking at the linguistic features of writing in this way can help to sharpen the focus of our teaching of writing: if we, as teachers, are clear about how a particular piece of writing is structured and shaped then we can address this more explicitly in our teaching. Moreover, this explicitness helps to give pupils access to metaknowledge about writing, demystifying the process and giving them access to the means by which their writing can be improved. The analysis of the A grade writer's pieces above also underlines how this can be developmental and formative, even for the most capable writers, because the targets for improvement can be articulated clearly and are both precise and attainable.

This discussion of these key factors in writing success deliberately illuminates how detailed consideration of the linguistic features of text can help describe success. However, it is not intended to provide recipes or formulas for successful writing which children are taught to adopt, nor is it intended to suggest that the teaching of writing should focus exclusively on these features. The importance of setting up writing effectively, helping writers to find something to say, and valuing what they do write is still of great significance. Attention to linguistic features is a natural complement to current best practice and enables teachers to be more focused in how they teach writing. We often talk about helping the child to find a voice. Perhaps in the past we have recognised neither the extent to which a child's voice can be lost or suffocated by poor understanding of how to craft and express ideas, nor the extent to which form and meaning are intrinsically inter-related.

PRINCIPAL TEACHING IMPLICATIONS FROM	
PUNCTUATION	**CLAUSE STRUCTURE**
◆ the avoidance of the comma splice (using a comma where a full stop is required) especially in narrative ◆ the differing functions of comma usage, including using commas for effect and to remove ambiguity ◆ the use of parenthetic commas ◆ the correct use of the possessive apostrophe ◆ the use of a wider range of punctuation devices, including the colon and semi-colon	Co-ordinated clauses: ◆ the use of effective co-ordination; ◆ avoiding excessive co-ordination; ◆ the use of alternative co-ordinators to *and* or *but*. Subordinate clauses: ◆ the use of subordinate clause structures; ◆ handling complex ideas through subordination; ◆ recognising tangled or confusing subordinate clauses; ◆ the use of a wider range of subordinators.

SPELLING
◆ unstressed vowel error and homophone error ◆ consideration of other semantic and syntactic cues to teach and improve spelling ◆ phoneme and letter omission, particularly at F grade ◆ elision and word breaks, particularly word breaks for higher achieving students ◆ consonant doubling

THE TECHNICAL ACCURACY PROJECT	
PARAGRAPHING	**TEXTUAL ORGANISATION**
◆ the tendency of F grade students to omit paragraphs in general and paragraphing of dialogue in particular ◆ the use of adverbials to link narrative paragraphs, with particular emphasis upon adverbials which link according to place ◆ the range of conjuncts used to link paragraphs in non-narrative and the evaluation and expansion of current use	◆ creating effective non-narrative openings ◆ creating effective endings in both narrative and non-narrative ◆ establishing and maintaining a relationship with the reader ◆ cohesion in narrative and non-narrative and the significance of pronouns and other language features in establishing cohesion

SENTENCES	**WORD CLASS**
◆ sentence length ◆ the use of short sentences for effect ◆ the use of simple sentences ◆ the avoidance of over-long rambling sentences ◆ achieving variety in length ◆ sentence structure ◆ appropriate co-ordination and subordination ◆ avoiding repetition of similar structures ◆ expansion and elaboration within the sentence	◆ The use of abstract nouns as an alternative to adjectives and adverbs, especially in narrative ◆ Increasing the ratio of lexical to non-lexical words

8   TEACHING WRITING

As the previous section indicates, one outcome of the recent research into writing is that it has become easier to illuminate aspects of writing that would benefit from teacher attention. The finding that there are many aspects of punctuation in this category will not come as a surprise to most secondary teachers, and difficulties with the possessive apostrophe can be thought of as a national malaise!

However, what is more important is how this research extends our professional conceptions of pupil difficulties into a range of more concrete areas for teaching. The grid on the previous page spread summarises the key features of pupils' writing in which teachers could usefully attempt to develop greater skill and understanding. There is a close relationship between these key features and the teaching objectives identified in the draft Framework for English Years 7-9, as the examples below, taken from the National Literacy Strategy Framework, indicate:

- expand nouns and noun phrases in a variety of ways e.g. by using a prepositional phrase – *the quiet man with the foolish grin*;
- deploy punctuation to clarify meaning, particularly at the boundaries between sentences and clauses;
- develop and vary the structure of sentences within a paragraph to lend pace, variety and emphasis appropriate to the content.

It is important to emphasise that these key features of writing are by no means exclusively concerned with accuracy. Even in the punctuation category, whilst inaccuracy with possessive apostrophes and with comma splicing are noted, other aspects of punctuation, such as the use of commas for effect and the use of the parenthetic comma are more intrinsically related to how the writer crafts a text to shape meaning. The notion of creating meaning is central to many of these teaching implications: the way subordinate clauses can support the expression of a complicated argument; the way different adverbials in narrative can enhance the reader's ability to engage with the narrative; the way pronouns can support or disrupt cohesion and so on. Underlying these findings is a pertinent reminder that good writers are more than accurate, and that accurate writers are not necessarily good writers – competence in writing is about crafting, shaping, manipulating and polishing language to achieve a desired effect.

In the remainder of this section, some of these teaching implications are explored in more depth with guidance on two different teaching strategies – scaffolding and modelling - which might enhance the teaching of writing. The danger of both the 'Teaching Implications' grid and the strategies which follow is that writing may become decontextualised from other aspects of the English curriculum; or that lessons focus on how to use parenthetic commas or adverbials, for example, without any reference to specific writing tasks in hand. The draft Framework for English Years 7-9 (NLS) reiterates the importance of objectives which are '*taught explicitly*' and which are '*identified and deployed in context*'. The opportunities for rooting explicit attention to these features of writing in language study which already occurs is rich and there is ripe potential for drawing attention to these features in reading texts and to parallels in oral activities.

USING FRAMES AND SCAFFOLDS

The teaching tool of the writing frame has now gained widespread familiarity through the work of Maureen Lewis and David Wray, and is a tool frequently used in the National Literacy Strategy. Superficially, a writing frame is a worksheet with prompts given to start each section of the writing. However, it is important to understand clearly why writing frames can be successful in offering support to apprentice writers and how they are deliberately designed to nurture children's learning.

As a means to support learning, the writing frame is rooted in the thinking of Lev Vygotsky, a Russian psychologist, whose ideas on how children learn have become highly influential. Many teachers reading this book will have been trained at a time when the dominant theories of how children learn were those of Jean Piaget. He believed that children progressed through age-related developmental stages and that it was not possible to teach a child something before they had reached the appropriate developmental stage. The idea of 'reading readiness' and non-interventionist teaching policies reflect this way of thinking. But Vygotsky is largely responsible for establishing a new way of thinking. He believed that language was the crucial factor in a child's development and that to progress a child needs support and guidance from an expert. Vygotsky maintained that for all learners there is a grey area, a zone, where we are unable to operate independently but can succeed if we are given structured support. The father who holds his toddling child's hands while she learns to walk and the driving instructor with dual controls are both examples of support being given to learners which helps them to learn how to become independent in an activity. To summarise the difference between Piaget and Vygotsky rather crudely, Piaget believed teachers shouldn't teach anything until pupils were ready for it, whereas Vygotsky believed teachers should help pupils move on one stage from where they where, and help them understand or do something they couldn't previously do.

The writing frame is intended to be the support which helps the learner move on and to develop confidence in attempting new forms of writing. By providing structural shape for a piece of writing it enables a writer to see the structural characteristics of that form, and the wording of the prompts frequently gives linguistic support in adopting the appropriate means of expression. In addition, the linguistic prompts help writers in gaining access to the *cohesive links* in a given type of writing. It acts as a scaffold for learning, which can be removed when the writer becomes more confident.

In the writing frame on the following page, devised to support the writing of an argument, the introduction and conclusion both give prompts to suggest the kind of ideas which are typical of introductions and conclusions. The introduction opens with a sentence which introduces both the topic of school uniform and the notion of argument, given that British children have to wear uniform whereas their European counterparts do not. Likewise, the conclusion offers a framework for drawing the argument together, *'taking other views into account'* and for concluding with an expression of the writer's own perspective.

On one level, the introduction and conclusion prompts offer content support – what to say – but on another level, they also offer structural support in understanding how openings and endings are managed in an argument piece. The ending, particularly, illustrates how the preceding arguments can be acknowledged, maintaining cohesion, before leading into a conclusion based on the writer's viewpoint.

IS WEARING A SCHOOL UNIFORM AND GOOD OR A BAD THING? WHAT DO YOU THINK?

In Great Britain, most school children have to wear school uniform, although this is not true on the Continent...

On the one hand, some people argue that we should keep school-uniform because...

Moreover, some people believe that...

However, on the other hand, there are those who would argue that...

Similarly, people also claim that...

Conclusion: Taking all the different views into account, my own opinion on this topic is ...

The prompts provided for the main body of the writing assist the writer in organising the arguments appropriately into points and counter-points, and furthermore, provides a structure for paragraphing. The words in the prompt are intended to give writers access to the vocabulary of argument: there are three different words used for *argue* (*argue, claim, believe*) and the conjuncts (*moreover, however, similarly, on the other hand*) support the cohesive connections between paragraphs and the ideas.

Although there are many writing frames now available for teachers to use at secondary level, the process of designing a writing frame for a given form or type of writing is illuminating. Often as teachers we know very clearly what the outcome of a writing task should be and we recognise good and poor writing when we see it. But designing a writing frame obliges us to think explicitly about how a text is structured and its typical linguistic features. What would a writing frame for a literary critical essay look like, or for a newspaper editorial, or for a book review? Thinking explicitly about our implicit expectations of a given writing type can inform the way we teach, enabling us to show writers how to be successful with greater clarity.

There are some dangers inherent in the use of writing frames, which are important to note at this point. In some ways, the writing frame has become a victim of its own success. Its popularity has led to a proliferation of frames and, at secondary level, the writing frame has also been adopted as a cross-curricular strategy for developing literacy. So, some Science Departments use writing frames to guide the writing up of science experiments and teachers of history are using writing frames to help writers structure evidence in their essays. For the child, this can amount to 'Death by Writing Frame'! There is a need to ensure that the repertoire of teaching strategies to support writing is not confined solely to the use of a writing frame.

A more serious weakness related to writing frames is concerned with how they are used. If they are used without a full understanding of the principles underlying them, they become little more than glorified work sheets, where pupils fill in the gaps without ever grasping the learning about writing that the frames were intended to promote. Outside of the English lesson, it is already common to see 'writing frames' which offer no real structural or linguistic support, and which require writers to complete the boxes. Rather than being a support, the writing frames have become a strait-jacket, confining language in boxes.

Within English lessons, the fundamental principle to remember is that the writing frames are intended to be temporary supports to help writers gain confidence in writing in a particular form in order to move on to independence. The frames are not an end in themselves – they are the means to an end.

The teaching implications of this are twofold. Firstly, when writing frames are used, teachers need to draw pupils' attention to the structural and linguistic features so that pupils can make connections between the words on the page and their significance as characteristics of that form. Secondly, teachers need to think about how to move pupils on to independence – perhaps by reducing the amount of support given in a writing frame, perhaps by discussing alternative wordings for the prompts, perhaps by asking writers to attempt to write without the prompt. Like the child's first steps without holding her father's hands, the writer's first attempts at writing may be clumsy and awkward, but these first attempts at independence are important parts of the process.

OTHER SCAFFOLDING DEVICES

Of course, there are many other ways to scaffold pupils' writing through providing structural support. The Point – Quotation – Analysis (PQA) approach which many teachers advocate in writing literary responses is one such example. It helps writers to understand that confident writing in this genre involves making a clear point, substantiating it with a textual reference, and then developing it through an analysis or elaboration of the initial point. Providing sub-headings for a piece of writing or a list of questions which need to be answered serve a similar purpose.

Title: Write about a place that is special to you?

Brainstorming:

The loft.... Silence
Interesting - never the same twice
Exciting - climbing around the chairs;
Old stuff; boxes; looking at the old stuff.
Bats - in the far corner; hanging
 upside down;
shadows skimming past.
Warm and cold - dull light
Reading in the loft
Fibreglass - ceiling beams
Mysterious

Another well-used strategy to scaffold pupils' learning about writing is to use spider diagrams or concept maps to support awareness of structure, especially coherence. An example of one year 8 writer's initial brainstorm is reproduced above. The technique of gathering initial ideas in lists or diagrams is a familiar method for opening up a writer's thinking about what he or she wants to stay. But, it is the next step which needs scaffolding in terms of developing confidence in writing. Many writers find it very hard to move from what they want to say into an organised, structured piece of writing and weak writing at both Key Stage 3 and GCSE is often typified by good ideas poorly organised.

Inviting pupils to re-order or cluster the ideas in a brainstorm into a concept map or spider diagram in which ideas are connected or inter-related provides a framework for thinking about paragraphing, coherence and the best route through a piece of writing. It supports writers in thinking about paragraphing as a way of organising ideas in a text, rather than thinking about paragraphing as a way of organising text on a page. The same year 8 writer's spider diagram is reproduced below.

SPIDER MAP

Loft description:
fibreglass padding
between the joists
water tank - suitcases
and boxes
slanting ceiling beams
light - soft gloom

Excitement of being in the loft:
climbing up - sitting
behind the chairs
old things - rummaging
through; exploring
dusty; mysterious

My Special Place

The bats:
squeaking - high pitched
noise
pipistrelle bats
shadows flitting past
hanging upside down
sharing the loft

The silence:
reading up there
sometimes cold,
sometimes warm
peaceful
world of my own

USING TEXTS TO MODEL WRITING

The possibilities offered by written texts for exemplifying the characteristics of effective writing are limitless and provide a powerful tool for making connections between reading and writing. The National Literacy Strategy advocates the use of modelling as a strategy for the shared and guided writing elements of the Literacy Hour and the guidance given to teachers concerning the range of appropriate teaching strategies for literacy teaching includes modelling. The draft Framework for English years 7-9 reminds teachers of the effectiveness of *shared reading and writing – in which the teacher demonstrates and models the process of comprehension or composition with the whole class'*.

The benefit of modelling writing through examining texts is that the learner can see how different effects are achieved in context, rather than simply listening to the teacher's advice on given features. Most children will be familiar with the recommendation to use more adjectives to create description but this generalises quite considerably. Looking at the way printed advertisements use pairs of adjectives coupled by 'and' and possibly alliterative (e.g. *soft and smooth*) or lists of adjectives in threes (e.g. *dark, crunchy and delicious*) offers the child strong guidance on how adjectives can be used, in this context, to persuade. In fact, advocating the use of adjectives for description in writing more generally is misleading as an examination of most descriptive passages often shows that description is conveyed through all the lexical word classes, not just adjectives.

A further benefit of modelling as a strategy to help children improve their writing is that after it has been discussed for its relevant characteristics, the text remains as a model for pupils to refer to whilst writing. Like the writing frame, it acts as a scaffold, supporting the developing writer whilst he or she explores new writing territory. We have been using this strategy with great success for many years in poetry writing, asking pupils to write their own haiku, or sonnets, or cinquains after explanation of the key structure and typical subject matter of each form. The time is ripe to exploit this technique with other forms of writing.

In the following sections, three different examples of using texts to model writing are described and explained. Each focuses on a different aspect of writing.

9 CLASSROOM PRACTICE 4

Focusing on linguistic devices to support argument

A year 8 class was working on a scheme of work tackling writing argument and had spent previous lessons discussing and researching topics about which they had strong opinions. In this lesson, the intention was to move from the content of the arguments to a consideration of how they could be communicated most powerfully. An article opposing capital punishment was used as the basis for this learning and an overhead transparency of the article was projected on to a whiteboard in the classroom. Together, using different coloured whiteboard markers, the teacher and the class discussed the devices this article uses to make its argument effectively.

Human Rights and Unspeakable Wrongs

Pierre Sané, AI secretary general, calls on Britain to lead the fight against the inhumanity of capital punishment

Imagine this scene. In a dusty desert town in the Gulf emirate of Abu Dhabi two men are tied to a post in what a court ruling called a 'crucifixion' before execution. It is now late afternoon and they have been hanging there for eight sun-blistered hours. Do not think it is an image snatched from Biblical times. For this, sparing a last-minute change of heart, was to have occurred this very month, less than five flying hours from Britain, in the small town of al Ain.

In the end, spared crucifixion, the two men were shot by firing squad before a crowd of 2,000. What does this cruel tableau say? To the inhabitants of al Ain, it may be thought to offer its own peculiar lessons of retribution and deterrence. But what will they learn from such a spectacle? That it is right to kill people who have killed in order to teach them that killing is wrong?

... Governments can perform no more serious an act than taking the life of one of their citizens. Has it taken two millennia for this simple truth to sink in?

The Observer

There are many techniques used in this article to establish and underline the basic argument against capital punishment, not all of which were addressed with this year 8 class. However, the following linguistic devices were directly discussed:

- the use of a short sentence with an imperative verb to open the piece;
- a direct address to the reader, demanding involvement;
- the use of a narrative technique to establish the argument;
- creating a strong visual image through description (*sun-blistered*);
- making an emotive appeal rather than a logical request;
- the use of present tense in the narrative to create immediacy, the sense that this is happening now;
- the shift to past tense to make the intellectual argument;
- the use of rhetorical questions to engage and position the reader;
- the variety in sentence length with short, simple sentences frequently directly addressing or challenging the reader;
- the ending: parallel sentences – statement followed by rhetorical question, emotively linking capital punishment with the crucifixion of Jesus and then handing the thinking over to the reader.

Following the discussion of the modelled text, the pupils returned to their own chosen topic of argument which they had previously researched. They had been given a free choice of topic so they could genuinely engage in an argument where their purpose was to persuade others to accept their line of argument. The pupils were asked to think explicitly about which linguistic devices they could incorporate into their pieces to strengthen their argument and make it more effective. Copies of the article were distributed to pupils to act as a scaffold while they were writing.

In the extracts below, it is easy to trace the influence of the modelled text. These writers have variously used imperative verbs, rhetorical questions, short sentences, present tense for immediacy, and the narrative description of a scene. Moreover these persuasive devices are not simply littered through the writing without purpose – the writers have understood how to use the devices in an appropriate and effective manner. The modelling activity has prompted more than mere copying. The large number who write about football violence reflects the fact that this series of lessons occurred during the 1998 World Cup Finals.

Just imagine how people would react if it was the foxes ganging up on the dogs... Fox hunting is wrong! Don't you agree?
Anna

Smoking is bad for your health... Why is this?...
Sally

Imagine you're in France. You're standing in the middle of a road. On one side of you is a group of supporters and on the other side is a group of supporters of another team. What do you do?...
Football hooligans are not footballs fans! If they were they would think about their actions and what they are doing to their country...
Make friends, not enemies!
Eva

Tear gas lands at your feet. An empty beer bottle just misses you. A brick is thrown. This is what it is like to be in a riot...
I have yet to meet one person who doesn't agree. Imagine again the scene of teargas, drunks and beer bottles and think what can be done...
Mark

Imagine the scene. Grandly dressed men and women mounted on fine looking horses charging through a forest with a pack of noisy blood hounds.
Karen

I am against the Grand National..
Why do it?... It's torture...
Next time you watch the Grand National just think about how the horses must feel, and picture yourself in their position...
Donna

Imagine your perfect life, money, fame, a family, royalty and a boyfriend...
Although this time, Prince Harry and Prince William were left out, Diana did not want them to be photographed...
Martin

Imagine the worst. 15th June 1998 the opening game for England. England a place of happiness, France a place of mourning...
If only they knew that the thousands of ticketless fans outside the ground were causing mayhem...
Dan

The pieces of argument writing these pupils produced are not perfect and it is clear that some pupils relied more heavily on the modelled text than others. It is important to note that these are pupils of average ability with typical weaknesses who are finding their feet in a new area.

So, it is not surprising that a considerable number chose to use the verb 'imagine' as an imperative verb, just as the modelled text had done, though there is variety in the way they do this. A caveat with the use of writing frames was that they can lead to dependence rather than independence: the same is true of a modelled text and the teacher's aim will be to help pupils recognise and adapt the linguistic devices to their own writing. In this selection of writing there is evidence that some writers can do this from the outset. Donna invites her readers to 'think' and 'picture', her own persuasive imperative verbs. For other writers, the movement from close dependence on a model to greater independence will need to be supported by the teacher.

It is worth noting that the modelled text can support writers at all levels. Many of the writers represented in the sample above were in the average and above average ability range but less confident writers were also able to understand and use some of the linguistic devices. In the extract below, Kara, a Special Needs pupil, uses a rhetorical question and a short, verbless sentence to answer it. Usually Kara's writing was a sequence of long, often unpunctuated sentences with little awareness of her reader. This piece was a significant improvement.

Rabbits are nice to eat and do you have to pay a lot of money? No, of course not.
Kara

10 CLASSROOM PRACTICE 5

Focusing on openings and endings in narrative

As noted earlier, the Technical Accuracy Project drew attention to the relative insecurity many writers having in closing their writing appropriately. The following activities were designed to help pupils understand a variety of possibilities which are available when thinking about how to begin and how to end a narrative piece. It is not essential to teach about openings and closure in tandem but, in these activities, looking at openings as well as endings highlights some of the ways in which closure relates to the opening. Unlike the previous example of modelling, where teacher and pupils together analysed a text, these activities model through inviting pupils to explore the texts first and arrive at the teaching points afterwards.

The class were given a set of four narrative openings, along with a guidance sheet to help direct their thinking about how the openings operate. Broadly speaking, the guidance sheet draws attention to some of the more common ways of opening a narrative and it also helps to provide substance for discussion of the openings when the task is complete.

Following the sheet, the extracts are reproduced together with space for pupil comment and an indication of the reflections that a teacher would seek to draw out from a class.

HOW DO WRITERS START THEIR STORIES?

In pairs, read each of the openings and use this sheet to explore how each writer decides to open the narrative.

Does the extract...	Yes/No	Give details - names, descriptions etc.
Introduce a character?	1 2 3 4	1 2 3 4
Use dialogue?	1 2 3 4	1 2 3 4
Describe a place?	1 2 3 4	1 2 3 4
Suggest a problem?	1 2 3 4	1 2 3 4
Introduce a theme?	1 2 3 4	1 2 3 4
Suggest a possible plot?	1 2 3 4	1 2 3 4

Waiting for the Rain

Sheila Gordon

The second thing Frikkie always did when he arrived at his uncle's farm for the school holidays was look for Tengo. But first, he would run around exploring his favourite places to make sure that nothing had changed.

He would go first to the barn where the bales of hay were stacked, yellow and sweet-smelling, to the roof. Then he would race across the yard to the cowshed and greet the cows by name, patting his favourites on their warm glossy haunches and stroking them between their calm, mild eyes as their tails twitched away at the flies buzzing in from the glaring sunshine outside. Sarie...Marie...Tessie - creamy white, highly pedigreed, and dignified - who yielded the most milk of the herd. His uncle, Oom Koos, had gone overseas, to Scotland, to buy Tessie. "Cost me a fortune but worth every penny," he always said as the buckets frothed up with her rich creamy milk under the supple black fingers of Timothy, Tengo's father, who was the boss-boy on the farm.

Your notes:

_____

_____

_____

_____

COMMENTARY:

- Past tense, third person narrative, omniscient narrator;
- Introduces the characters of Frikkie and Tengo;
- Suggests a close relationship because the first thing Frikkie does is 'look for Tengo';
- Reveals a servant-master relationship in 'boss-boy' – Tengo's skin colour is introduced in 'supple black fingers' of Tengo's father;
- Rural farm setting established. A perceptive reader may use wider knowledge of world to pick up Oom Koos as an Afrikaans name and locate the setting in South Africa;
- An implied problem is apartheid or racial difference.

Why the Whales Came

Michael Morpurgo

"You keep away from the Birdman, Gracie," my father had warned me often enough. "Keep well clear of him, you hear me now?" And we never would have gone anywhere near him, Daniel and I, had the swans not driven us away from our pool under Gweal Hill where we always went to sail our boats.

Your notes:

_____

_____

_____

_____

_____

_____

_____

_____

COMMENTARY:

- Uses dialogue as first element in opening and moves to first person narrative, past tense;
- Introduces two characters, Daniel and the first person narrator – but it also introduces the Birdman, with the hints of danger and the clear warning from Gracie's father;
- A possible plot is suggested, implying that the narrative will recount what did happen when they disobeyed the father's warning and went near the Birdman;
- The setting is not a strong feature, though specific reference is made to Gweal Hill.

Skellig

David Almond

I found him in the garage on a Sunday afternoon. It was the day after we moved into Falconer Road. The winter was ending. Mum had said we'd be moving just in time for the Spring. Nobody else was there. Just me. The others were inside the house with Doctor Death, worrying about the baby.

Your notes:

_____
_____
_____
_____
_____
_____
_____
_____
_____
_____

COMMENTARY:

- First person narrative and past tense;
- Establishes that the narrator is part of a family, they have just moved, and that he/she has found '*him*' in the garage;
- The opening short sentence implies the significance of this discovery and suggests the narrative plot may revolve around '*him*';
- The absence of a name for '*him*' increases the mystery;
- A possible theme is suggested in the reference to the baby and Doctor Death.

Harry Potter and the Philosopher's Stone

J. K. Rowling

Mr and Mrs Dursley, of number four, Privet Drive, were proud to say that they were perfectly normal, thank you very much. They were the last people you'd expect to be involved in anything strange or mysterious, because they just didn't hold with such things.

Mr Dursley was the director of a firm called Grunnings, which made drills. He was a big, beefy man with hardly any neck, although he did have a very large moustache. Mrs Dursley was thin and blonde and had nearly twice the usual amount of neck, which came in very useful as she spent so much of her time craning over garden fences, spying on the neighbours. The Dursleys had a small son called Dudley and in their opinion there was no finer boy anywhere.

Your notes:

_____

_____

_____

_____

_____

COMMENTARY:

- Past tense third person narrative – omniscient narrator. Establishes a great deal about the characters, their names, their relationships, their physical appearances – and tells us that Mrs Dursley is nosy, and implies they both dote on their son;
- Their ordinariness is emphasised by the unassuming name 'Dursley', by the stereotypically suburban address and by Mr Dursley's job making drills;
- A possible plot is implied in the reference to the Dursleys' normality and their being the most unlikely people to be involved in anything *strange or mysterious*.

11 CLASSROOM PRACTICE 6

Focusing on closure in narrative

The second activity in this example of modelling is to shift the attention to closure. The closing lines of each of the four novel openings already studied were handed out and pupils were asked firstly to match the opening to the ending, and to discuss how they were able to make this decision.

Although names of key characters can be deleted in an exercise like this (such as *The Birdman* and *Frikkie*) it is useful to keep the names, as the echoing of characters in openings and endings is itself one device of cohesion. If pupils have matched an opening and an ending just by matching characters, then they need to be encouraged to think about other features which link the opening and the ending. Using the features investigated on the coding frames for textual organisation (see Appendix 1), it is possible to devise a set of questions to support pupils' thinking about how the narrative is concluded.

HOW DO WRITERS END THEIR STORIES		
1.	Does the story resolve a problem, or tie up loose ends, or leave the reader with something else to think about?	*show evidence of closure or resolution (including deliberate ambiguity)*
2.	Is the story still dealing with the same topic and still in the same genre?	*show congruence with genre/theme*
3.	Are there any words or ideas in the ending which echo the opening?	*echo/make reference to opening and/or developed context*
4.	Is there any final message, moral or viewpoint expressed?	*produce a coda, or comment upon theme*

Again, the extracts are reproduced together with space for pupil comment and an indication of the reflections that a teacher might draw out from his or her class.

Your notes:

_____

_____

_____

_____

_____

COMMENTARY:

- The ending suggests a resolution in the reference to Frikkie keeping his word and the underlying implication that this promise guarantees safety;
- There is some ambiguity: the character is returning home, safe, but there is still a sense of threat;
- One difficulty, with Frikkie, may have been resolved but a more general difficulty may remain;
- The ending sustains the third person narrative and Frikkie and another character, who we guess is Tengo, are still principal protagonists (though there has been a shift in viewpoint, from Frikkie's to Tengo's);
- The implied South African setting of the opening is reiterated in the reference to 'townships' and the colour problem echoed in the identification of Frikkie as a 'white soldier' and 'one of them'.

Why the Whales Came

Michael Morpurgo

Everyone drank from the well on Samson that day as if it were the elixir of life, and after that no one ever doubted the Birdman's story, not in my hearing anyway.

* * *

If you ever do go to the Isles of Scilly, go over to Samson and look around for yourself. The old ruined cottages are still there, a mound of limpet shells outside each one: and you'll find a well full of water. No one lives there, so you'll have only the terns and the black rabbits for company. You'll be quite alone.

Your notes:

_____

_____

_____

_____

_____

_____

COMMENTARY:

- The story starts and ends with references to the Birdman, but the opening warning has become a resolution – '*no-one ever doubted the Birdman's story*';
- The implied danger has become a happy ending with everyone united in drinking of the '*elixir of life*';
- The genre is still a first person narrative ('*my hearing*') and the Birdman evidently remains a central figure;
- The opening references to '*boats*' and '*Gweal Hill*' has been developed to the Scilly Isles marine setting;
- There is a coda after the resolution of the narrative – a comment that the island of Samson (the Birdman's island, perhaps?) is a place of solitude.

Skellig

David Almond

I watched her walk away in the late light. From across the street, Whisper came to join her. When Mina stooped down to stroke the cat, I was sure I saw for a second the ghostly image of her wings.

Back in the kitchen, they were talking again about giving the baby a proper name.
'Persephone,' I said.
'Not that mouthful again,' said Dad.
We thought a little longer, and in the end we simply called her Joy.

Your notes:

_____

_____

_____

_____

COMMENTARY:

- The ending resolves the problem of the parents worrying about the baby, introduced in the opening , and the baby's name, Joy, emphasises the happy outcome;
- A parallel but more ambiguous tying up of loose ends is implied in the mysterious reference to Mina's wings, perhaps a connection with the mysterious *'him'* of the opening;
- The idea of Doctor Death in the opening is replaced by the naming of the baby as 'Joy'; apart from the sustained first person narrator, the baby is the only character explicitly mentioned in the both opening and ending.

Harry Potter and the Philosopher's Stone

J. K. Rowling

'Hope you have – er – a good holiday,' said Hermione, looking uncertainly after Uncle Vernon, shocked that anyone could be so unpleasant.

'Oh, I will' said Harry, and they were surprised at the grin that was spreading over his face. 'They don't know we're not allowed to use magic at home. I'm going to have a lot of fun with Dudley this summer...'

Your notes:

_____
_____
_____
_____
_____
_____
_____
_____
_____
_____

COMMENTARY:

♦ Hermione's reference to a forthcoming holiday and to parting, and Harry's references to *summer* and *home* suggests the resolution of series of events framed by a school term and friendships at school;

♦ The reader might guess that the unpleasant Uncle Vernon is the beefy Mr Dursley of the opening, and we know from the opening that Dudley is his much-beloved son;

♦ The reference to magic echoes the Dursleys' dislike of anything strange and mysterious, mentioned in the opening, and allows the reader to imagine the narrative action continuing beyond the time frame of this book.

12   CLASSROOM PRACTICE 7

Focusing on textual organisation

The use of modelling as a supportive strategy for young writers does not have to make use of published texts exclusively. Modelling can be very effective when a teacher's own writing is used. In the example which follows, the teacher models the thinking process she follows in trying to organise text and exemplifies it through showing examples of initial ideas and organisation, as well as the completed piece. This strategy is sometime known as metacognition, whereby thought processes are revealed to learners so they can understand the process of writing more clearly. Put simply, it is a form of thinking aloud, letting learners into your head as a writer and hearing your explanations of how and why different decisions were made.

Textual organisation, especially cohesion and paragraph linking, are not always easy to teach and certainly have often been omitted from teaching about writing altogether. How initial disparate ideas can be structured into a coherent piece is a difficult concept to grasp. For the most confident writers, ideas tend to synthesise and crystallise fairly easily into an organised whole but, for many writers, the transition from initial ideas into writing is painfully difficult, In personal writing, one consequence is frequently narratives with little sense of a reader, propelled by chronological narrative action.

Through modelling her own approach to writing and through discussing the characteristics of the finished piece, a teacher can begin to foreground attention on some of these difficult processes. Using an overhead transparency with key questions and examples of initial ideas and structural outlines, the teacher can talk through a piece of writing and how she approached structuring it. In the example below, the teacher's metacognitive 'thinking aloud' is represented in speech marks, though in practice, of course, this would not be scripted. The example does not deal with drafting and editing: these are significant processes in themselves and are ideal for this kind of modelling. But, because the focus in this activity is how to move from random ideas to some kind of organising structure, the attention to drafting is best set aside for another lesson.

After modelling the process of gathering and organising ideas, the teacher would use her finished piece as a model to highlight its organisational features. In this case, the teacher would draw attention to the way paragraphs are linked, echoing previous ideas and moving them on, and the way the piece moves from the general to the specific, and from the past to the present. She could also usefully highlight where the piece adds to or deviates from the original outline.

The task asks the writer to describe a situation when he or she was very frightened and in approaching it, the teacher sets out to pose three questions. How would I think about this writing task and what would I do first? What would I do next? How would I tackle the actual writing?

THINKING ABOUT THE TASK - WHAT WOULD I DO FIRST?

	BRAINSTORMING
'The first thing I would do is to gather some ideas so that I have something to work on. I would think hard about a real time or situation when I was very frightened, trying to picture the scene and recall the details. Then I would write down/brainstorm all my recollections, ideas, feelings related to this time. My immediate thought on being asked about a time when I was frightened is to write about my fear of the dark as a child.'	Fear of darkness ◆ *Running downstairs with feeling that something is chasing me* ◆ *In bed at night- hands dangling out of bed - serpents under bed* ◆ *Going to outdoor toilet in Ireland - animal shadows; total blackness;* ◆ *Bedroom at night - dressing gown swinging on door is like a ghost* ◆ *Words/feelings: terror; lurking; menace; threat;*

WHAT WOULD I DO NEXT?

'The next thing I would do is to look at all my initial ideas and see if I can think of an effective way to shape this into a piece of writing? I would ask myself: Do I need to include all these initial ideas? How might I start the writing? Is there one idea which sounds more interesting than the others? Then I would try to decide on an outline of the structure of the piece which would help me to organise my ideas and plan a route through the piece of writing.

With this title and these initial ideas, I decided that I would start with a general introduction explaining my fear of the darkness and giving some examples of typical situations where I feel frightened (probably trying to give this a touch of humour). But the main body of the writing would focus on the way I can feel frightened in the darkness of my own bedroom. I would describe some of the situations in my bedroom that make me feel frightened, and then write about my childhood fear of serpents under the bed. This would be the principal element of this piece of writing and I would describe both the situation and the serpents in some detail. I might end by revealing that I am still frightened of imaginary serpents under the bed!'

My outline structure is below:

Introduction:

A description of my general fear of darkness; over-active imagination; running downstairs; Irish toilet etc.

Worst fear of darkness occurs in bedroom - strange shadows; wallpaper patterns; toys come alive; creatures at window; dressing gown becomes a ghost.

Particular incident: serpents under bed; early childhood - fear of being bitten by serpents under bed - read lots of stories about snakes and serpents.

The serpents - describe the imaginary serpents.

Conclusion

I still can't hang my hands out of bed!

HOW WOULD I TACKLE THE WRITING?

'I would start writing using my outline notes as a guide, though I would be prepared to incorporate new ideas and alter things slightly as I write. You never really know exactly what you want to write until you start writing! I would try to add plenty of detail as I write – descriptions of the darkness, of the bedroom, of the serpents - and I would want to make sure I included information about my feelings. I would try to make it a little bit humorous – after all, my fears are all pretty silly, though very real.

The outline structure would help me with paragraphing, either by writing one paragraph per numbered point; or several paragraphs per numbered point, depending on how detailed the final piece became. I would think about how each paragraph will link with the previous one, perhaps through contrast, or through echoing an idea or a word in the previous paragraph, or through introducing a new idea related to my fear of the darkness.

As I write, I would try to keep my reader in my mind and imagine the effect my writing might have upon him or her. I would like an ending which links my childhood fears with me today because fears are powerful things."

My final piece of writing, after revision and editing, might have looked like this.'

Monsters in the Dark

For as long as I can remember the darkness has filled me with fear and has energised my active imagination into over-drive. As the daylight fades, the darkness seems to invade the house, taking over like a silent army, filling every corner with silent horrors. The menace is tangible.

I can recall many, many evenings where I would hurtle down the stairs at top speed, convinced that someone, or even worse, something was following me. One of the worst experiences in the dark repeated itself every time we went on holiday to my grandmother's farm in Ireland.

The old farmhouse had no inside toilets and at night I would have to walk across the farmyard to a rotting wooden cubicle, hounded at every step by monsters waiting in the shadows.

But the worst fears always came to life in my own bedroom. At night the room changed character and personality. Dolls formed threatening shadows and lost their gentle daytime appeal. My dressing gown, pale white in the darkness, glimmered like a ghost and any movement would set it quivering with alarming reality. Even the patterns on the wallpaper assumed a life of their own and could shrink, expand or shiver in the darkness. The only safety lay in clutching my teddy very tightly and hiding under the bedcovers.

However, the night time horrors of the bedroom were not just a feature of infancy. By the time I was about ten I had grown sufficiently to lie with my arms dangling over the side of the bed. But this presented the worst horror of all - the serpents waiting under the bed, waiting to bite. I loved reading, and many of the stories told of dangerous snakes with venomous bites and serpents who could perform untold terrible deeds.

I knew the serpents were there under the bed. When it was very quiet, I could hold my breath and hear their secret wriggling and writhing in the dark space under my bed. I could picture their long bodies, rainbow-sequinned, intertwining and twisting around each other. From their mouths, black forked tongues flicked with anticipation and beady eyes gleamed. My flesh recoiled at the thought of the feel of their dry, scaly skin. And I knew they were waiting - waiting for the careless moment when I would forget, and let my arms dangle helplessly over the edge of the bed.

To this day, I cannot sleep with my arms hanging out of the bed.

13 WORKING WITH GENRE

How does the detailed work on aspects of language set out in the previous sections link to the genre and writing types specified in the National Literacy Strategy, the English national curriculum, the draft Framework for Key Stage 3 and the national GCSE syllabuses?

Firstly, the expectations placed on writers under each of these headings - and the prescribed criteria for success - embed these aspects without ever making them explicit. For example and in their most recent manifestation, the targets set for writing by the end of Year 9 expect the individual child to become a confident writer, able to:

- write for a variety of purposes and audiences, knowing the conventions and beginning to adapt and develop them;
- write imaginatively, effectively and correctly;
- express, experiment with and manipulate sentences;
- organise, develop, spell and punctuate writing accurately.

Secondly, as in this example, the expectations are mixed so that purpose and audience jostle with choices about convention. There is an almost deliberate absence of clarity about such statements and teachers often claim to have absorbed them to the extent that they can recognise 'good' persuasive writing, for example, without being able to precisely identify what makes such writing effective. Even GCSE marking schemes are unable to be more specific, so that 'best' writing is frequently revealed by the indicator that it is 'well matched to purpose and audience' or uses 'appropriate conventions' without ever setting out what these are.

Thirdly, the picture is made more complicated by what almost amounts to a fudging at Key Stage 3 between the non-fiction writing types set out in the National Literacy Strategy for Key Stage 2 and the writing 'triplets' used for assessment at Key Stage 4 and GCSE.

In the National Literacy Strategy at Key Stage 2, there are six non-fiction writing types. As these are introduced to classes within the teaching framework, some of their linguistic and stylistic characteristics are identified in addition to notions of purpose and, to a lesser extent, audience. The main features are as shown in the chart below.

WRITING TYPES IN THE NATIONAL LITERACY STRATEGY			
Type or Purpose	Language Features	Whole text features	Criteria for Success
Information Text	◆ use of the present tense and third person	◆ information is organised and linked	◆ the effective incorporation of examples
Recounting	◆ the use of the past tense ◆ temporal connectives	◆ maintain, clear chronology	◆ the understanding of past events given to a reader
Explanation	◆ present tense and an impersonal voice	◆ logical and causal connections	
Instruction	◆ The use of imperative verbs	◆ helpfully sequenced and signposted	◆ the quality of guidance provided to the user
Persuasion		◆ sentence syntax used to emphasise points	◆ the use of links in a developing argument
Discursive Writing		◆ signposts the organisation of contrasting points	◆ an attempt to clarify a viewpoint expressed

In contrast, there are twelve writing types at GCSE level which are organised into four groups, each containing three types or 'triplets'. These are:

- ◆ imagine, explore, entertain;
- ◆ inform, explain, describe;
- ◆ persuade, argue, advise;
- ◆ analyse, review, comment.

In practice, these are forms of, or purposes for, writing rather than writing types. The chart below gives examples of types of writing under each heading and draws out some global links between them. It also underlines the potential range of writing under that 'fits' each heading and indicates that there are some critical linguistic distinctions to be drawn between the 'grouped' purposes.

WRITING TYPES AT KEY STAGES 3 AND 4		
PURPOSE	**LINKING FEATURES**	**WRITING EXAMPLES**
◆ **imagine** ◆ **explore** ◆ **entertain**	*organised by subject, narrative development relying on chronology*	◆ stories, diaries, reflections ◆ playscripts or poems ◆ autobiographies, screenplays, adaptations, experimentation
◆ **inform** ◆ **explain** ◆ **describe**	*organised by topic, sequential or chronological development, direct address to unknown reader*	◆ memos, minutes, summaries, information leaflets ◆ accounts, records ◆ plans, prospectuses, instructions
◆ **persuade** ◆ **argue** ◆ **advise**	*organised by theme, direct address to specific reader*	◆ leaflets, pamphlets, posters and commercial advertising ◆ letters, magazine articles
◆ **analyse** ◆ **review** ◆ **comment**	*organised by theme or group, focus on readers in general*	◆ discursive essays, reports ◆ book, film and stage reviews ◆ articles, commentaries

On the following pages, the numbered objectives set out in the Key Stage 3 Framework for each triplet and for Years 7-9 are brought together to give an overview of the form (the numbering is as in the Framework). They are then placed alongside some suggestions for a teaching focus linked to particular aspects of language, hints on assessment, and some key phrases for teachers who wish to develop their own frames to match particular writing tasks.

IMAGINE, EXPLORE, ENTERTAIN

YEAR 7 Pupils should be taught to:

1. structure a story with an arresting opening, a developing plot, a complication, a crisis and a satisfying resolution;

2. portray character and motivation, directly and indirectly, through description, dialogue and action;

3. use a range of narrative devices to involve the reader;

4. experiment with different forms, styles and genres to present similar material, and compare the results;

5. experiment with the visual and sound effects of language, including the use of imagery, alliteration, rhythm, rhyme;

6. use writing to explore and develop ideas.

Language Features that can be taught:

♦ Openings and Endings;

♦ Changing sentence length to influence narrative pace;

♦ Conjuncts or adverbials that are other than time-related;

♦ Reader asides and added detail within parenthetical commas;

♦ The use of dialogue and correct punctuation;

♦ Reader-writer relationship.

YEAR 8 Pupils should be taught to:

1. use language experimentally to explore ideas, emotions and imaginative experience;

2. explore different ways of opening, developing and ending narratives and evaluate their impact on readers;

3. experiment with narrative perspective;

4. explore different language choices to establish tone;

5. experiment with writing in the style of a range of writers they have read;

6. explore the visual and sound effects of language in a variety of poetic forms and styles.

Additional Assessment Focuses

♦ Cohesion: use of tenses, names and pronouns;

♦ Clauses: Use of subordination;

♦ Word Class: Choice and use of adjectival and adverbial description;

♦ Whole text: Attainment of relationship with reader.

YEAR 9 Pupils should be taught to:

1. entertain the reader by developing an imaginative or unusual treatment of familiar material;

2. reveal character, establish settings and develop narrative through an effective mix of action, dialogue, description and commentary;

3. write within the discipline of different poetic forms, identifying how form constrains and contributes to meaning;

4. write playscripts and/or short screenplays which explore and exploit the presentational conventions of drama and film;

5. explore how non-fiction texts can amuse and entertain.

Key Headings for Frames

♦ An exciting opening ...

♦ Setting the Scene ...

♦ Moving the plot forward ...

♦ A character description ...

♦ Increasing the pace ...

♦ Including dialogue ...

♦ The climax ...

♦ The ending ...

INFORM, EXPLAIN, DESCRIBE

YEAR 7 Pupils should be taught to:

7. select and present information in a way that is appealing and accessible to its target audience;

8. explain a process logically, highlighting the links between cause and effect;

9. give instructions and directions which are specific, easy to follow and clearly sequenced;

10. describe an object, person or setting in a way that is both accurate and evocative;

11. organise texts in ways appropriate to their content, and signpost this clearly to the reader;

12. use detail, example, diagram and illustration, as appropriate, to illustrate meaning.

YEAR 8 Pupils should be taught to:

7. organise and present information selecting appropriate material and making effective use of language, layout and illustration;

8. write a balanced explanation of an event or issue which reflects and represents a range of evidence and opinions;

9. articulate abstract ideas or emotions;

10. convey a sense of character and/or setting through the selective use of detail, imagery or implication.

YEAR 9 Pupils should be taught to:

6. integrate diverse kinds of information into a coherent account, using formal and impersonal language;

7. explain complex processes and ideas effectively and economically in print or on screen;

8. explore and develop the use of description in different kinds of text.

Language Features that can be taught:

♦ Establishing the context for the writing;

♦ Making logical links in stepped explanation particularly with conjuncts or adverbials which order or sequence;

♦ Establishing prior knowledge in instruction;

♦ Offering definitions using parenthetical commas for specialised terminology;

♦ Using adjectival and adverbial description;

♦ Using the imperative for instructions and directions;

♦ Using the passive voice if appropriate;

♦ Tense consistency in explanation and description.

Additional Assessment Focuses

♦ Cohesion: paragraph links that develop or contrast effectively;

♦ Clauses: Use of adverbial or non-finite to define, exemplify or develop;

♦ Word Class: Choice and prior explanation of specialist vocabulary;

♦ Punctuation: use of lists, charts, bullet points or colons;

♦ Whole text: Attainment of clear focus on reader and his or her needs.

Key Headings for Frames

♦ My context is …

♦ The first stage is …

♦ Next, you should …

♦ Then, …

♦ Finally …

PERSUADE, ARGUE, ADVISE

YEAR 7 Pupils should be taught to:

13. express and develop a personal view with clarity;

14. in presenting ideas, anticipate the needs, interests and views of the intended reader;

15. add emphasis to key points;

16. use a range of strategies to validate an argument.

Language Features that can be taught:

♦ Use of the Imperative and conditional (if .. then) constructions;

♦ Brainstorming and spider diagrams as aids to planning;

♦ Using topic sentences to signal direction of argument;

♦ Conjuncts and conjunctions in paragraph linking;

♦ Appeals to reader using parenthetical commas.

YEAR 8 Pupils should be taught to:

11. develop and defend a personal view, using appropriate rhetorical devices;

12. present a counter-argument to a view that has been expressed, addressing weaknesses in the argument and offering alternatives;

13. clarify and convey in their own writing the difference between knowledge, belief and opinion;

14. give written advice which offers alternatives and takes account of the possible consequences.

Additional Assessment Focuses

♦ Cohesion: use of repetition for effect, conjunct variety;

♦ Clauses: Use of co-ordination for assertion and subordination for supporting arguments;

♦ Word Class: Control of imperative and direct address;

♦ Punctuation: use of semicolons and colons;

♦ Whole text: Address to reader and use of rhetoric, vocabulary and information.

YEAR 9 Pupils should be taught to:

9. present a personal view with clarity and conviction;

10. use persuasive techniques and rhetorical devices to gain the attention, and influence the responses of readers;

11. develop and signpost arguments in ways that make the logic clear to the reader and anticipate responses and objections;

12. offer general advice, or guidelines for action, illustrated through particular examples.

Key Headings for Frames

♦ I think that... , In my view ..., However ...

♦ What if ...

♦ What you should do first is ...

♦ Before deciding you should think about ...

♦ One possibility would be ... Another would be ...

♦ So, to sum up my view is ...

♦ Have you ever thought about ...

♦ Some people say ... but I think ...

ANALYSE, REVIEW, COMMENT

YEAR 7 Pupils should be taught to:

17. identify criteria for evaluating a particular text, object or event, present findings fairly and give a personal view;

18. plan, write and present a critical review for a specific audience, and revise it in the light of their response.

Language Features that can be taught:

♦ Use of introductory paragraph to set context;

♦ Point, Evidence, Comment framework for paragraphs;

♦ Conjuncts, modal verbs and phrases to convey tentativeness, contrast and conclusions;

♦ Vocabulary of evaluation and comparison, particularly verbs;

♦ Concluding summative paragraphs.

YEAR 8 Pupils should be taught to:

15. explore the differences between formal analysis and personal commentary;

16. evaluate a process or product in relation to agreed criteria;

17. identify and use the features of reviews which are appropriate for different readers;

18. weigh different viewpoints and present a balanced overview of an event or issue.

Additional Assessment Focuses

♦ Cohesion: conjunct variety, management of tenses;

♦ Clauses: Use of subordination for speculation;

♦ Word Class: verb variety to express and reflect;

♦ Punctuation: use of commas to present alternatives or contrasts;

♦ Whole text: Ability to sustain a point of view, to make conclusions based on evidence offered.

YEAR 9 Pupils should be taught to:

13. present a balanced analysis of a topic, taking into account a range of evidence and opinions;

14. cite detailed textual evidence to justify critical judgements about texts and their overall impact;

15. comment on complex or controversial texts or ideas in ways that reflect the significance of the subject matter for the readers.

Key Headings for Frames

♦ In this essay, I intend to …

♦ On the one hand … , on the other …

♦ It should now be clear that …

♦ Many people believe that …

♦ A further possibility is …

♦ It can be argued that …

♦ In conclusion, my own view is that …

14 USING ICT TO IMPROVE WRITING

The potential of new technology in general and the new school subject, Information and Communications Technology (ICT), in particular for developing pupils' writing is enormous. This section cannot hope to explore all of the possibilities but it is important in a book about improving writing to emphasise the role that technology can play in school and the role that it already has in the workplace. Virtually all writing in commerce, industry and public services is now realised through the use of a computer, be it printing bills and invoices, or writing letters and reports.

Therefore, the children we teach today are certain to use their writing skills in a technological context once they leave school. The truth is that the chances of them using pen and paper for extended writing are probably quite slim. What is more new word-processing and publishing software – the categories are emergent and fluid - is not only facilitating writing but is also changing the process. Fixed templates used for certain writing types, such as business letters, reports, action plans and so forth are, in their own way, ready-made writing frames, supporting and guiding the structuring of writing.

Also, as many people compose directly onto the screen and the speed and ease of editing on screen makes it possible to draft and re-draft work repeatedly, the notion of the final – finished - product becomes increasingly elusive. Indeed, to some extent the word-processor has already eroded the finality of a 'final' copy: work can always be changed further and the notion of work in progress now includes the final copy. Examination board requirements for drafts of coursework, for example, now seem archaic and contrived.

From the perspective of the classroom and this book, however, the key question is how can we tap the potential of ICT to teach better writing? It is perhaps unfortunate that one of the principal ways computers are used in English has been to produce best copies of writing on a word-processor. Probably every English teacher is familiar with the piece of writing laboriously typed into a word-processor, often containing more errors than the original, and printed in an inappropriately large font because the piece seemed so much shorter once word-processed than on school paper.

One issue this raises is that of the need for fluent and accurate keyboard skills in order to exploit the facilities that a word-processor can offer but it also highlights that the computer is often seen principally as a presentation device, a means to produce neat and attractive work. This can indeed be a valuable asset, especially to the child with untidy handwriting or physical disabilities and should be exploited where appropriate but in the context of teaching writing it is the 'alterability' of text on screen which is of greater significance. The computer allows the writer to edit, to experiment, to keep different versions of work, to move text around, and to insert additional text in a way that simply is not possible with pen and paper.

There are, of course, resourcing implications. The availability of technological resources varies from school to school as does the kind of access which English teachers may have to these resources. The teaching implications of access to a computer per child as opposed to one computer per teaching room are quite considerable. However, access to computing facilities is improving and there are already schools that have electronic whiteboards in their classrooms which make the sharing of model texts and work straightforward. With one of these, whole class work on editing or sharing the process of analysis on a modelled text is made easy. Likewise, the extent to which English teachers have direct access to the Internet should expand to open up a vast range of possibilities for publishing pupils' writing, or for arranging peer discussions with writers in other schools, or other countries.

Electronic white boards and 'always on' internet connections are for the future. Rather than dealing with advanced resources which many schools may not have, this section will address how the most basic of word-processing facilities can be used to enhance the teaching of writing. The word-processor allows the teacher to set up a wide variety of activities which invite writers to explore and investigate text, and to manipulate and alter text on screen to consider various effects.

Overleaf is a list of ten activities which teachers can adapt to encourage writers to think about how writing is crafted and shaped. Many of them lend themselves to paired work where access to machines is limited. The first two examples are outlined in more detail in Appendix 3.

15 CLASSROOM PRACTICE 8

Working with ICT on writing. Copy these pages for use by colleagues. Assess the effectiveness of the approaches.

Sentence Variety

Using extracts from a selection of novels, count the number of words (using a Word Count tool) and the number of sentences and calculate the average sentence length. If pupils are confident with the concepts of simple and multiple sentences, they can also count the occurrence of these in the extracts. Discuss the reasons for some of this variety (such as how the use of dialogue often creates short sentences and pre-twentieth century texts often have some very long sentences) and discuss the effects of different sentence lengths and types.

Conjuncts

To develop confidence in using conjuncts in persuasive or argument writing, draw up a table with three columns headed *Summarise, Contrast, Add Extra Information* and ask pupils to cut and paste or drag the listed conjuncts into the appropriate column. Then, ask pupils to try to use some of them appropriately in their own writing.

Paragraphing

Using either an effective piece of writing by one of the class or a published piece, highlight the first sentence of a paragraph and discuss how that sentence links back to the previous paragraphs; and how it moves the ideas forward, perhaps by developing an idea, by introducing a new idea, or by contrasting an idea. When the idea is established ask class to undertake a similar analysis.

Cohesion & coherence

Using the Font colour button, trace vocabulary chains/ideas/themes through a piece by highlighting different chains or themes in different colours. As above, teach the method then let the class try to do the same.

Narrative voice	Rewrite a first person narrative in the third person (or *vice-versa*) and consider what effect this change has upon the writing. This technique can sometimes help weaker writers who become so involved with a personal narrative they cannot distance themselves from it and consider the needs of the reader. Rewriting narratives in an altered tense (past into present, for example) can provoke a useful discussion about literary effects.
Changing the type of text	Rewrite a given text as a different type of text (e.g. a recipe as a science experiment). Then compare the alterations to arrive at a clear understanding of the linguistic features of each (e.g. imperative verbs in the recipe; passive voice in the experiment; the importance of ordering and sequencing ideas in both.)
Narrative structure	Using a story that is short enough to fit on one screen page, order unsequenced paragraphs into a coherent narrative. Discuss the narrative structure of the piece.
Excessive co-ordination	Using an example of a pupil's work which contains too much co-ordination, highlight the co-ordinators. Pupils can be asked to highlight *and, but, or* if they are uncertain about the grammatical terminology. Alter the passage to include fewer co-ordinators, not just by deleting and putting in full stops, but also by considering the use of some subordinators (*while, as, because, although, unless, if…*)
Closure in argument writing	Using a published or teacher written argument piece without its final paragraph, ask pupils to write the conclusion. Give prompts to shape their thinking, such as how does your ending link with the opening; how does it link with the ideas expressed in the piece; how does it provide a summary or a clear expression of your viewpoint. Print all the conclusions and in groups discuss how successful the various conclusions are.

Using pupils' own writing, particularly if pupils are regularly repeating the Subject-Verb-Object pattern, invite them to look at their sentence structure and to experiment with varied sentences. Try beginning a sentence with an adverb (*silently, surprisingly, effortlessly*); or with an adverbial (*beneath the stars; by the shore; later that night*). Further playing with sentence structure could include reversing the main clause – subordinate clause order so that the subordinate clause is fronted, and using a non-finite clause to start the sentence (*Loved by all his friends, Charlie...*)

With all these activities involving ICT, it is obviously important to root them in a unit of work which is addressing that particular type of writing. Otherwise, there is danger that they become little more than decontextualised writing exercises. The discussion which accompanies or follows the activity is central to ensuring that pupils make explicit connections between what they are doing on screen and what they are learning about writing. The transfer of learning from screen to pupils' own writing is supported by using a variety of texts as the focus of study, from published texts, to teacher-written texts and pupils' own work. If pupils are composing on screen, the potential for developing differentiated tasks that address specific writing needs for individuals in the context of their own writing is greatly increased.

16 MAKING BETTER ASSESSMENTS

Although the principal benefits of exploring the linguistic features of writing relate to teaching, there are many ways in which assessment can be informed by a fuller understanding of the linguistic characteristics of text. More understanding of linguistic techniques represents enhanced subject knowledge for English teachers, building on and adding to the understanding of literary techniques. This additional knowledge allows for an increasingly perceptive response to children's writing, in both summative and formative approaches to assessment. As the Key Stage 3 Framework for English: Years 7-9 expresses it, 'The best assessment has an immediate impact on teaching because it alerts the teacher to the needs of pupils who are either out of step or exceeding expectations'.

PRESENTATION	SURFACE FEATURES	CONTENT	STRUCTURE
◆ handwriting ◆ use of ICT ◆ visual layout ◆ illustrations	◆ spelling ◆ punctuation	◆ themes ◆ punctuation ◆ vocabulary coherence ◆ ideas	◆ opening ◆ paragraphing ◆ cohesion ◆ closure
▼	▼	▼	▼

Purpose

Audience

Form

In assessing children's writing, it is helpful to be consciously aware of the spectrum of responses available. The past criticism of teachers' tendencies to mark only spelling and punctuation is a familiar argument, and few English teachers now would be found making comments which relate only to spelling and punctuation (although there are still many children who nonetheless pick up a message that neatness and good spelling and punctuation are the most important features of writing). The table above offers a reminder of the spectrum of English skills as they might be deployed in an effective piece of writing. There is an argument that in terms of language development and learning this is the key diagram that teachers need to have in their heads, or refer to, in planning lessons and schemes of work.

ASSESSING EFFECTIVENESS IN WRITING

The same diagram can also be useful in discriminating between aspects of writing which need to be addressed at an early stage of planning and drafting, and aspects which might be better addressed at a later stage. Revising the spelling and determining an appropriate form of presentation are part of the final stages of the writing process, whereas organising the structure and the content are much more organically related to the act of composition. It is a mistake, which many writers make, to think that paragraphing, for example, can be sorted out after a text has been written. This can only be successful if the writing already has a clear cohesive organising principle underlying it, otherwise the insertion of paragraph breaks becomes a superficial layout convention unrelated to the internal logic and structure of the piece.

The inclusion of punctuation in both the surface features and the content columns serves as a reminder that punctuation is a meaning-making convention, as well as a text-marking convention. Checking that proper nouns are appropriately capitalised, that dialogue is correctly demarcated, or running a final check through the writing to look for comma splices can be undertaken in the later stages of writing. However, there are many ways in which the punctuation and the composition inter-relate or intersect: the use of direct addresses to the reader in persuasive writing is supported by the parenthetic comma; the decision not to use contractions to create a more formal tone; the use of a comma to mark off a clause for emphasis, for example. In these cases, the punctuation is more than the accurate application of text-marking conventions, and relates more to the creation of meaning than to accuracy.

Confident knowledge of linguistic characteristics in text enables teachers' responses to address the sub-elements of this table with considerable specificity and precision, and helps to avoid the pitfalls of making responses which appear to acknowledge only one or two aspects of a child's writing in fairly general terms.

Summative assessment is a primary concern for teachers but while our intuitive judgements as English teachers about the relative merits of a piece of writing are often correct they may well be qualitatively unsubstantiated or generalised. Examiner meetings, inset sessions and writing workshops – the opportunities for teachers to reflect on marking strategies - which invite explanations of why a piece of writing is strong or weak, stimulate some familiar responses. So, the writing is credited because it:

- ◆ *has an interesting vocabulary;*
- ◆ *is appropriate for its purpose;*
- ◆ *engages the reader's interest;*
- ◆ *has an authentic voice;*
- ◆ *is accurately written – syntax, spelling and punctuation;*
- ◆ *is well-organised.*

These, of course, are precisely the characteristics which we would hope to find in a good piece of writing and useful as 'shorthand' but they are nonetheless generalised. There is no substantiation of 'interesting' vocabulary, or any indication of how the reader's interest is engaged, for example. Yet, as previous chapters have demonstrated, it is possible to be very precise and explicit about the ways in which vocabulary is interesting and the effects it achieves, or about the techniques the writer uses in order to engage the reader's interest. Closer analysis of the linguistic features of a child's writing can permit substantive flesh to be put on these intuitive bones, and can be a powerful tool for making judgements. The following example of a capable primary school writer from year 3 indicates how a recognition of the vitality and energy of this young writer's piece can be assessed with some precision.

What can be said about this piece? It would be easy to comment positively on the writer's enthusiasm, they way he has imported information from a history lesson effectively, and the authenticity of his account. However, in reality, there is much more here to be unpacked.

So, the writing uses sentences of varying length, including short sentences for impact ('*I woke up. I didn't want to get up.*') and simple sentences with direct clarity ('*My dad is a trader and a farmer*'). The longer, complex sentences shift from explanation of the narrator's experience to explanation of the setting and context ('*We live...our land*').

YEAR 3 BOY: NARRATIVE

I woke up. I didn't want to get up. Such warm bracken and old deerskins stuffed with feathers. Time to get the firewood for brekfast. Yum, yum - bacon and fried hens' eggs. Oh no, the cows are eating our roof!! 'Cows, stop it!' Mm - the nice smell of wood smoke and more food for the grown-ups. Now my horse, sword and spears are being preapared for helping dad and loads more to hunt down food... My dad is a trader and a farmer. We live in a little clearing surrounded by water so we go across by my dad's best longship or by a little dinghy to deliver wepons and supplies because lots of people feel safe on our land.

In addition, the type and structure of the sentences are varied. There are several verbless sentences for effect, emphasising the boy's feelings about his experiences and creating a sense of immediacy which draws the reader's interest (' *Such warm bracken...*') . The sentences are not all straightforward Subject-Verb-Object sentences beginning with a noun or a pronoun, and one sentence includes a passive construction ('*Now my horse, sword and spears are being preapared..*') which brings the key information to the front of the sentence. The passage shifts from past tense to present tense, a shift which is not wholly successful.

The writer provides his reader with plenty of detail to understand the setting and also to understand the narrator's responses to this setting. There is expansion around the finite verb to locate or explain events: there are non-finite clauses - '*to hunt food*' ; '*surrounded by water*'; and adverbials - '*in a little clearing; ' on our land*'; and adjectival premodification *(warm; old; fried; nice; little; best; little)*. The nouns in this piece are particularly well-chosen. Many of the nouns are topic-specific and help the reader to establish the time setting/historical context of the writing *(deerskins; firewood; sword, spears; weapons; longship)*. It is noticeable that the adjectives are the least effective feature of this writer's ability to create descriptive detail. In general, the adjectives are selected from a more ordinary vocabulary repertoire, whilst the nouns, non-finite clauses and adverbials do most of the descriptive work. A further feature of the vocabulary is the use of informal, colloquial vocabulary, ('yum, yum'; 'loads'; 'mm').

Overall, this passage is varied and lively, evoking a clear sense of the historical time frame, of the scene being described, and the narrator's perspective on it.
A summative assessment such as the one above, which is only looking at a small extract from a longer passage, illustrates how close attention to the text's structures and the use of different word classes can begin to explain how the text is succeeding or falling down. From the assessment, formative feedback can be given which relates most appropriately to the writer's immediate needs. Below, three of the points which could be picked up with the writer are discussed. Note that assessing writing in this way is not simply about finding fault, but equally about identifying success and making that success explicit to the writer. The notion of implicit and explicit knowledge is important. Writers may demonstrate a facility for using a particular feature because they have implicitly understood its significance. Explicit understanding is more likely to lead to conscious repetition of a successful technique, and, in the long term, to the conscious rule-breaking which so often characterises the very best writing.

EFFECTIVE FEEDBACK

♦ Discuss the *verbless sentences* – were these deliberate or accidental? Talk through the impact of the verbless sentences and how they succeed in intensifying the experience through omission of the verb. Perhaps, consider also whether there are too many. There are four.

♦ Make explicit *the way the writer has added detail* – through *topic specific nouns*; through *adjectives*; and through *non-finite clauses* and *adverbials*. Note especially how the topic-specific nouns work to establish the historical context and provide appropriate detail.

♦ Talk about *time and tense* – the immediacy of the present; the recount/recall of the past – the need to be consistent.

♦ Talk about *formality and informality*: the inappropriacy of 'loads more'; the effect of 'yum, yum' and 'mm'.

With less confident writers, it is often a temptation to respond only to the weaknesses in spelling and punctuation which mar a piece of writing, because they are so apparent. Greater awareness of other features of text can sometimes enable a teacher to recognise the strengths of a weaker piece. There is considerable difference between the writer who organises a narrative effectively, uses a lively vocabulary, engages the reader's interest through provision of detail or suggestion of a narrative problem but makes abundant spelling and punctuation errors, and the writer who has struggled to communicate the gist of a narrative, and who has little awareness of the needs of the reader, and who also makes abundant spelling and punctuation errors. Sometimes, these writers receive similar judgements from their teachers.

A further advantage of an appreciation of the linguistic characteristics of text in making summative judgements is that it can sometimes enable recognition of the cause or causes of a less successful piece. Knowing, for example, that the weakest writers tend to use no adjectival description at all, whilst writers who are becoming more confident use adjectives as their principal means of description, and confident writers use a greater repertoire of descriptive devices, including adverbials and non-finite clauses, gives a new perspective on typical middle range writing. It becomes possible to see precisely why this kind of writing, heavily dependent on adjectives, reads rather dully.

Although in the above the emphasis is on summative assessment, a detailed reference to textual features makes assessment – almost inevitably - formative. This is made more explicit when the effective use of an understanding of the linguistic features of writing in informing formative assessment is dependent upon an inter-relationship between teaching and assessment. More simply, if the teaching of writing has adopted strategies which illuminate explicitly various linguistic characteristics then the possibilities for building on this in formative feedback are rich. It introduces a shared language, a way to talk to children about writing, which can be developed and enlarged as the child's understanding progresses.

There is a type of writing, common in many middle ability secondary age writers, which although technically accurate is rather flat and uninteresting. Frequently, it is this kind of writing which teachers find it hardest to respond to effectively as there are no obvious technical points to note, and nothing of particular merit to praise. In workshop sessions, teachers often report that their comments on this kind of writing are rather bland and unfocused. An example of this kind of writing is reproduced below. It is an extract from an empathic piece written in response to the poem, *La Belle Dame sans Merci* by John Keats.

YEAR 8 BOY: NARRATIVE

I was riding on my horse to day when I saw the girl of my dreams. She had long blond hair and a perfectly shaped face. My knees started to knock together and I started to sneeze. I was sure I had made a mess of it so I asked her her name. She just put her finger to her lips and said nothing. I didn't know what to do so I walked away. I sat and thought for a while before I decided to make her a garland. I went back to where I first found her and as I got there I started sneezing again.

At face value, this piece is spelled and punctuated correctly and is a simple chronological narrative of an emotionally significant event. But the narrative is undeveloped and unconvincing, leaving the reader with many unanswered questions (not least, why was he sneezing?) Assessing the writing with a closer focus upon its linguistic features begins to explain why it is less successful and, equally important, offers clear pointers to how the piece could be improved.

The rather flat tone is created by the heavy use of finite verbs to convey the narrative action and by the use of a considerable amount of co-ordination. There are nineteen finite verbs in this piece, compared with nine in the year 3 boy's account of life during Viking times. This dull tone is reinforced by a highly repetitive sentence structure. There are no short sentences for emphasis and the sentences are of similar length. All the sentences begin with a pronoun, often *I*, and all the sentences consist of a main clause followed by a subordinate or co-ordinate clause.

There is remarkably little detail provided about the setting, the context or the narrator's emotional response. There are few adjectives, the exception being the description of the

girl (*long blond; perfectly shaped*). The nouns are drawn
from an everyday repertoire and are fairly commonplace
(*horse; girl; hair; face; name; mess; finger; lips...*). The
exception is *garland* which is the one word in the piece
which gives a slight hint that this is not set in contemporary
times. The verbs are also commonplace, and given the
reliance on the verbs to maintain the narrative, they add
little in terms of detail or description – the repetition of
started three times is a weak point.

The reference to '*the girl of my dreams*' and the allusions to
knocking knees signal the emotional import of this
encounter, but, tantalisingly, there is no elaboration,
explanation or authorial reflection upon this. There is also
some uncertainty in the coherence: does the girl remain
stationary on her horse while the boy goes away *for a while*
and makes a garland? This is a piece of writing waiting to
get out!

EFFECTIVE FEEDBACK

♦ Highlight the over-dependence on finite verbs and illustrate how
  to add more detail through non-finite clauses, adverbials and
  adjectives. This could be achieved through annotating questions
  onto the writing. Where were you? How did you feel? What was
  she doing?

♦ Discuss the repeated sentence structure and demonstrate
  simple ways to vary them e.g. Putting an adverb or a non-finite
  clause at the start of the sentence (*Knowing I had made a mess
  of it, I asked her name; Immediately my knees started knocking
  together...*)

♦ Circle all the co-ordinating conjunctions and discuss how they
  contribute to making the narrative move too fast at the expense
  of narrative reflection or authorial comment. Encourage the
  writer to alter some of the co-ordinated sentences, perhaps by
  using a subordinator instead e.g. *Because I didn't know what to
  do, I walked away, disappointed.*

♦ Consider how the lexical vocabulary could be altered to
  heighten the historical and folkloric setting of the piece (e.g.
  maiden; lady; enchanting; knight). The writer could be
  encouraged to draw more on Keats' vocabulary which helps to
  set the scene and mood (*steed; faery; pale; sigh; fading; elfin*)

Looking closely at the linguistic features of writing enables formative feedback to be sharper and more relevant to the writer's needs or the demands of the task. In the case of middle ability writers like this one, formative feedback as indicated below can help the writer to find his voice and to understand how to communicate more effectively through the written medium.

A further way of using linguistic analysis alongside literary analysis to inform the assessment of writing is to establish appropriate targets for improvement. This could follow naturally from the teacher's assessment of a piece of writing and subsequent discussion with the writer. So, in the case of the year 8 writer above, the targets for improvement might include asking the pupil to try to:

- reduce dependence on finite verbs by adding more detail within the sentence;
- avoid overuse of co-ordination;
- vary the length of sentences, with some short sentences for emphasis;
- vary the structure of sentences, avoiding repeated use of S-V-O sentences, by fronting adverbials, non-finite clauses or subordinate clauses;
- consider how the choice of vocabulary adds detail and specificity concerning setting, emotions and the time frame for the writing.

Alternatively, the target-setting could be built upon establishing shared criteria for success, which are discussed with writers prior to beginning a writing task and which form the basis of the final assessment. These criteria could be collectively constructed through study of a modelled text and analysis of its linguistic and literary features.

One way is to use 'success ladders'. The two examples of success ladders on the next page were designed for writers to self-assess their own writing using the right-hand column, followed by the teacher's assessment using the left-hand column. The first ladder uses generic criteria which would be appropriate to any piece of writing, while the second is task-specific, devised following the analysis of a modelled text.

GENERIC CRITERIA FOR PUNCTUATION		
T	**SUCCESS CRITERIA**	**S**
yes	uses speech marks correctly	**yes**
no	uses varied devices e.g. colon	**?**
(yes)	uses parenthetic commas	**?**
yes	uses commas to mark clauses	**yes**
yes	uses commas for lists	**yes**
no	uses capital letters for proper nouns	**yes**
yes	uses capital letters to start sentences	**yes**
yes	uses full stops correctly	**yes**

TASK-SPECIFIC CRITERIA FOR WRITING NARRATIVE		
T	**SUCCESS CRITERIA**	**S**
yes	opening establishes theme	**yes**
yes	opening introduces time frame, character or setting	**yes**
no	well-chosen verbs for action	**?**
yes	evidence of descriptive detail	**yes**
no	evidence of authorial reflection or comment	**no**
yes	paragraphs used	**yes**
no	paragraphs linked well	**yes**
yes	closure links with previous text	**yes**
yes	closure resolves theme	**yes**

17 APPENDIX 1

The Technical Accuracy Project

In 1996, QCA (then SCAA) commissioned an investigation into writing in GCSE English examinations. The Technical Accuracy Project (TAP) as it was called, spanned three years, culminating in the final report, published by QCA in 1999 (*Technical Accuracy in writing in GCSE English: research findings*, QCA, 1999). The first stage of the project was to develop and trial a series of coding frames which would permit a detailed analysis of children's writing and provide data which would be constructive and useful.

The consequence of this stage of the project was the evolution of six coding frames, investigating six different aspects of writing. The six coding frames investigated were:

◆ spelling;
◆ punctuation;
◆ Non-Standard English usage;
◆ clause structure and word class usage;
◆ paragraphing;
◆ textual organisation.

From the outset, there was a commitment to looking at writing from several perspectives: from the word level (spelling) to sentence level (punctuation; clause analysis, Non-Standard English) to whole text level (paragraphing; textual organisation). In addition, the analysed samples were taken from both narrative and non-narrative text types to allow comparisons between the two. Overall, the investigation focused upon three characteristics of writing. These were:

◆ accuracy;
◆ effectiveness;
◆ patterns of usage.

Pupils' **accuracy** in spelling, in correct use of sentence punctuation, in paragraphing and in the use of Non-Standard English was measured. Their **effectiveness** in handling clauses, in linking paragraphs, and in whole text features, such as cohesion and establishing a reader-writer relationship, was recorded. A final layer of analysis looked at

patterns of usage of linguistic features and devices, such as commas, adjectives, and conjuncts to link paragraphs.

The writing used for the investigation was drawn from the QCA archive of GCSE English scripts. 144 scripts were used representing four examination boards and an even balance of A, C and F grade pupils. An attempt was made to achieve a gender balance, but in the event this was only possible at grades A and C, as the archive of F grade candidates was predominantly from boys. For each candidate, two pieces of writing were used, one narrative and the other non-narrative.

So precisely what kind of writing features did these coding frames explore? The tables on the following pages summarise the scope of the analysis in each coding frame. They can be used diagnostically by teachers or departments to analyse samples of writing from school pupils and to identify any consistent patterns of weakness.

CODING FRAME FOR CLAUSE AND WORD CLASS ANALYSIS

Clause analysis	Number
Number of sentences: defined by grammatical structure, rather than punctuation	
Number of finite verbs:	
Co-ordinated clauses: Count the number of co-ordinating devices e.g. *and/but/so/and then/neither...nor* Include the comma as a co-ordinating device if appropriate	
EFFECTIVENESS RATING:	1 2 3 4
Subordinate clauses: e.g. *time; place; cause; purpose; relative; condition*	
EFFECTIVENESS RATING:	1 2 3 4

Word class analysis	Number	Actual words used
Abstract nouns		
Other nouns (excluding proper nouns)		
Adjectives (exclude *some, very, many, much, a lot/lots,* and numbers)		
Adverbs		
Non-lexical words: prepositions; conjunctions; articles; auxiliaries		
Comment on the impact of the clause structure, verb choices and word class usage. *Note especially how sentence structure, co-ordination and subordination are effectively handled, or whether the vocabulary used is imaginative, adventurous or particularly apt.*		

ANALYSIS OF NON-STANDARD FEATURES USED IN WRITING

DO NOT COUNT NON-STANDARD USAGE IN DIRECT SPEECH *(leave box in blank if you find zero)*	Number present	Please write actual examples of Non-Standard usage below
Non-Standard irregular past tense forms: e.g. *shooted; breaked*		
plural subject with singular verb: e.g. *they goes*		
singular subject with plural verb: e.g. *he shoot well, doesn't he?*		
Use of is/was after there with plural nouns: e.g. *there is/was lots of people*		
adjective used as adverb: e.g. *He did it quick*		
Non-Standard irregular past participle forms: e.g. *I was sat*		
more with comparative adjective: e.g. *more quicker*		
use of preposition in place of verb e.g. *should of; could of*		
Non-Standard use of prepositions: e.g. *I went up the shops*		
me with subject Noun Phrase: e.g. *Me and John*		
no plural marker on nouns of quantity, measurement &c: e.g. *five pound of apples*		
Non-Standard use of definite/indefinite article:		

CODING FRAME FOR THE ANALYSIS OF SPELLING

Total number of words correctly spelled:	

Range and sophistication of the vocabulary used: (3: most sophisticated, please circle)

1 2 3

Type of Error	Errors in sample (write down each example)	No.
omission: of -d, -ed or -ing on verb or participle		
omission: of s on plural form or on verb		
omission: phonemes (other than s, or ed or ing)		
omission: other single letters		
ending: -s, -ing or -ed added to words ending in Y		
ending: verbs which end in e: adding -ing or other		
ending: adverb formation error with -ly or -ally		
ending: other suffix formations (e.g. -ful, -able, -ible)		
sound: homophones		
sound: error in long e formation		
sound: errors in unstressed vowels		
sound: phonetically plausible		
sound: hard/soft consonant error		
other (1): elision, word division		
other (2): inversions		
other (3): consonant doubling - inflections		
other (4): consonant doubling - all other		
other (5): common words		
other (6): implausible, illegible		

CODING FRAME FOR THE ANALYSIS OF PARAGRAPHING: NARRATIVE

Total number of paragraphs: (where there is no paragraphing enter '0')			

Use of paragraphs or other layout devices (please tick)	Appropriate		Partly appropriate	Absent

Is dialogue used? (please tick)	YES / NO	If yes, is paragraphing (please tick)	Appropriate	Partly appropriate	Absent

Continue the analysis only if paragraphing is present.

Are links between paragraphs shown by:	Number	Notes/examples	
use of conjuncts (ordering) or adverbials (time) (e.g. *later; meanwhile; later that day; after a while; finally; when they saw the body; at 10 o'clock, etc.*)			
adverbials (place) (e.g. *in the garden; back at the ranch etc.*)			
other linguistic patterning (e.g. *repetition of verbs or significant nouns, or refrain*)			
structural patterning (e.g. *events in plot, chronology, shifts or patterns in character or place; thematic patterning*) Please tick	STRONG EVIDENCE	SOME EVIDENCE	LITTLE EVIDENCE
Any comments, particularly on structural patterning			

CODING FRAME FOR THE ANALYSIS OF PARAGRAPHING: NON-NARRATIVE

Total number of paragraphs: (where there is no paragraphing enter '0')			

Use of paragraphs or other layout devices (please tick)	Appropriate	Partly appropriate	Absent
Use of paragraphs or other layout devices (please tick)	Appropriate	Partly appropriate	Absent
Other layout devices used (please tick)	Subheadings	Bullet Points or Numbers	Quotations
Where paragraphs are used, are they introduced by a topic sentence or statement of theme? (please tick)	Mostly	Sometimes	Never

Is dialogue used? (please tick)	YES / NO	If yes, is paragraphing (please tick)	Appropriate	Partly appropriate	Absent

Continue the analysis only if paragraphing is present.

Are links between paragraphs shown by:	Number Occurring	Notes/ examples
use of conjuncts - listing, ordering e.g. *firstly; secondly, finally, to summarise, once, later, meanwhile, after that, then* (or phrases whose function is to list or order)		
use of conjuncts - contrasting, re-focusing e.g. *however, on the other hand, moreover* (or phrases whose function is to contrast or re-focus)		
other linguistic patterning e.g. *repetition of key words; repetition of a verbal technique*		

structural patterning e.g. *logical development of subject or theme; logical contrast of subject or theme* (please tick)	STRONG EVIDENCE	SOME EVIDENCE	LITTLE EVIDENCE

Any comments, particularly on structural patterning:

CODING FRAME FOR TEXTUAL ORGANISATION: NARRATIVE WRITING

In the first ten lines or opening paragraph, evaluate the writer's ability to:

produce an effective opening	1 2 3 4 Comments
signal the genre/theme, either explicitly or implicitly	1 2 3 4 Comments
establish or leave clues to context: character/setting/time frame	1 2 3 4 Comments
initiate the narrative 'problem'	1 2 3 4 Comments

In the final ten lines or closing paragraph, evaluate the writer's ability to:

produce an effective ending	1 2 3 4 Comments
show evidence of closure or resolution (including deliberate ambiguity)	1 2 3 4 Comments
show congruence with genre/theme	1 2 3 4 Comments
echo/make reference to opening and/or developed context (character/setting/time frame)	1 2 3 4 Comments
produce a coda, or comment upon theme	1 2 3 4 Comments

In the whole text, evaluate the writer's ability to:	
establish a relationship with the reader	1 2 3 4 Comments
position the reader appropriately via rhetorical questions, asides, statements and questions, use of passive or active voice	1 2 3 4 Comments
position the reader appropriately via emotive or judgmental lexis	1 2 3 4 Comments
support the reader by maintaining control of narrative through use of pace and detail	1 2 3 4 Comments
sustain or develop viewpoint	1 2 3 4 Comments
In the whole text, evaluate the writer's ability to:	
maintain cohesion/coherence	1 2 3 4 Comments
maintain cohesion (e.g. via use of names, pronouns, ellipsis, reference to assumed knowledge, tense)	1 2 3 4 Comments
maintain coherence (e.g. by sustaining narrative, character, setting, theme, genre)	1 2 3 4 Comments
reinforce plot/theme (e.g. via repetition or contrasts)	1 2 3 4 Comments
sustain lexical harmony	1 2 3 4 Comments
Make a judgement about the overall quality of the textual organisation; ring the appropriate number	1 2 3 4 Comments

NOTE: 1 2 3 4 For each point below circle one number (4 = highest quality)

CODING FRAME FOR TEXTUAL ORGANISATION: NON-NARRATIVE WRITING

In the first ten lines or opening paragraph, evaluate the writer's ability to:

produce an effective opening	1 2 3 4 Comments
signal the theme/topic	1 2 3 4 Comments
signal the genre/form, for example through use of verb tense or subject (abstract, generic, personal, non-personal)	1 2 3 4 Comments

In the final ten lines or closing paragraph, evaluate the writer's ability to:

produce an effective ending	1 2 3 4 Comments
show congruence with the opening	1 2 3 4 Comments
show congruence with the theme/topic	1 2 3 4 Comments
show congruence with the genre/form	1 2 3 4 Comments
provide a clear summary or conclusion	1 2 3 4 Comments

In the whole text, evaluate the writer's ability to:	
establish a relationship with the reader	1 2 3 4 Comments
position the reader appropriately via address (direct or indirect), register (formal or informal), modality, use of passive or active voice	1 2 3 4 Comments
position the reader appropriately via affective or judgmental lexis, use of rhetorical devices	1 2 3 4 Comments
manage content/information/evidence (on behalf of the reader)	1 2 3 4 Comments
sustain or develop a point of view or argument	1 2 3 4 Comments

In the whole text, evaluate the writer's ability to:	
maintain cohesion/coherence	1 2 3 4 Comments
maintain cohesion (e.g. via use of pronouns, ellipsis, conjuncts, tense)	1 2 3 4 Comments
maintain coherence (e.g. by sustaining theme or form)	1 2 3 4 Comments
reinforce argument/theme (e.g. via repetition or contrasts)	1 2 3 4 Comments
sustain lexical harmony	1 2 3 4 Comments
Make a judgement about the overall quality of the textual organisation	1 2 3 4 Comments
NOTE: 1 2 3 4 For each point below circle one number (4 = highest quality)	

18 APPENDIX 2

Auditing writing in Schemes of Work for English

The copymaster on the facing page can be reproduced for use in your own school. You can download a PDF file containing all of the charts and tables in the appendices from the Courseware Publications website.

www.courseware-publications.co.uk

ENGLISH SCHEME OF WORK AUDIT

Title of Scheme of Work:

Year Group:

Aims of Scheme of Work:

- to
- to
- to

Writing Task	Purpose	Teaching focus	What will be assessed?

Total number of writing tasks:

Total number of tasks with explicit focus on writing skills

EVALUATION:

19 APPENDIX 3

Using ICT to Develop Writing

The copymasters on these pages can be reproduced for use in your own school. You can download a PDF file containing all of the charts and tables in the appendices from the Courseware Publications website.

www.courseware-publications.co.uk

USING ICT TO EXPLORE SENTENCE LENGTH IN NOVEL OPENINGS

	Number of words	Number of sentences	Average no. of words per sentence	No. of simple sentences	No. of multiple sentences
Jane Eyre					
Junk					
Great Expectations					
Northern Lights					
The Tulip Touch					

WHAT TO DO:

When you have completed the first table, copy and paste the shortest sentence in each extract and the longest sentence in each extract into the second table (next page). Can you think of any reasons why these openings vary so much in sentence length and type? Now look at the opening to your own narrative piece and try out the same activities. How long are your sentences? How varied are your sentences? What effects are you trying to create?

	LONGEST AND SHORTEST SENTENCES
Jane Eyre	S: L:
Junk	S: L:
Great Expectations	S: L:
Northern Lights	S: L:
The Tulip Touch	S: L:

ICT: OPENINGS USED IN THE SENTENCE LENGTH ANALYSIS

from 'Jane Eyre' by Charlotte Bronte

There was no possibility of taking a walk that day. We had been wandering, indeed, in the leafless shrubbery an hour in the morning; but since dinner (Mrs Reed, when there was no company, dined early) the cold winter wind had brought with it clouds so sombre, and a rain so penetrating, that further outdoor exercise was now out of the question.

I was glad of it: I never liked long walks, especially on chilly afternoons: dreadful to me was the coming home in the raw twilight, with nipped fingers and toes, and a heart saddened by the chidings of Bessie, the nurse, and humbled by the consciousness of my physical inferiority to Eliza, John, and Georgiana Reed.

The said Eliza, John, and Georgiana were now clustered round their mamma in the drawing-room: she lay reclined on a sofa by the fireside, and with her darlings about her looked perfectly happy.

from 'Junk' by Melvin Burgess

A boy and a girl were spending the night together in the back seat of a Volvo estate car. The car was in a garage. It was pitch black.

'I'm hungry,' complained the girl.

The boy turned on a torch and peered inside a grey canvas rucksack behind him. 'There's an apple.'

'Nah. Any crisps left?'

'Nope.'

Gemma sighed and leaned back in the car. She pulled a blanket over herself. 'It's cold,' she said.

'Barry'll be here soon,' Tar said. He watched her closely in the torchlight, frowning anxiously. 'Sorry you came?' he asked.

Gemma looked over and smiled. 'Nah.'

Tar snuggled up against her. Gemma stroked his head. 'You better save the batteries,' she said in a minute.

Tar turned off the torch. At once it was so black you couldn't see your own hand. Surrounded by the smell of damp concrete, oil and petrol, they carried on their conversation cuddling in the dark.

Tar said, 'Come with me.'

from 'Great Expectations' by Charles Dickens	My father's family name being Pirrip, and my Christian name Philip, my infant tongue could make of both names nothing longer than or more explicit than Pip. So, I called myself Pip, and came to be called Pip.

I give Pirrip as my father's family name, on the authority of his tombstone and my sister - Mrs Joe Gargery, who married the blacksmith. As I never saw my father or my mother, and never saw any likeness of either of them (for their days were long before the days of photographs), my first fancies regarding what they were like, were unreasonably derived from their tombstones. The shape of the letters on my father's gave me an idea that he was a square, stout, dark man, with curly black hair. From the character and turn of the inscription, 'Also Georgiana, Wife of the Above', I drew a childish conclusion that my mother was freckled and sickly. |
| *from 'Northern Lights' by Philip Pullman* | Lyra and her daemon moved through the darkening hall, taking care to keep to one side, out of sight of the kitchen. The three great tables that ran the length of the Hall were laid already, the silver and the glass catching what little light there was, and the long benches were pulled out ready for the guests. Portraits of former Masters hung high up in the gloom along the walls. Lyra reached the dais and looked back at the open kitchen door and, seeing no one, stepped up beside the high table. The places here were laid with gold, not silver, and the fourteen seats were not oak benches but mahogany chairs with velvet cushions.

Lyra stopped beside the Master's chair and flicked the biggest glass gently with a fingernail. The sound rang clearly through the Hall.

'You're not taking this seriously,' whispered her daemon. 'Behave yourself.' |

from 'The Tulip Touch' by Anne Fine

You shouldn't tell a story till it's over, and I'm not sure this one is. I'm not even certain when it really began, unless it was the morning Dad thrust my bawling brother Julius back in Mum's arms, and picked up the ringing telephone.

'The Palace? Why ever would they want me at the Palace?'

Anyone listening might have begun to think of royal garden parties, or something. But even back then, when I heard people saying things like 'the black horse' or 'the palace', I got a different picture. And that's because I've lived in hotels all my life. I don't even remember the first one, the Old Ship. Mum says it was small and ivy-covered, with only six bedrooms. Then Dad was manager of the North Bay. And later he was moved to the Queen's Arms, where we were living then.

USING ICT TO EXPLORE CONJUNCTS AS PARAGRAPH LINKS IN WRITING TO ARGUE

Use the CUT and PASTE facility to sort these conjuncts into categories under the appropriate heading according to whether you think they summarise information, contrast information, or add extra information.

SUMMARISE	CONTRAST	ADD EXTRA

consequently
to conclude
finally
secondly
overall
on the other hand
moreover

alternatively
likewise
however
therefore
equally
nevertheless
whereas

Go back to your original piece of argument writing and look at how your paragraphs link with each other. Now develop, expand or amend your writing using some of the conjuncts above. Think carefully about whether you are trying to contrast ideas, add extra information or details about similar ideas, or whether you are trying to sum up.

20 APPENDIX 4

Writing and Thinking Skills

The recent emphasis on Thinking Skills is closely linked to the development of the Draft Framework for Years 7-9 where it is argued that English teachers have a significant part to play in nurturing them. The subject is viewed as presenting possibilities in several areas that relate to the use of thinking skills in writing but, perhaps particularly, in terms of organisation and reasoning.

The chart below draws together the information on thinking skills for each of years 7-9. It is interesting to see how whole text features of writing relate to these, and how any kind of assessment of thinking skills, based on these objectives, would need to draw on a detailed analysis of aspects of language and writing.

	YEAR 7	**YEAR 8**	**YEAR 9**
Information Processing	Wr19 collect, select and assemble ideas in a suitable planning format. Wr8 explain a process logically, highlighting the links between cause and effect. Wr11 organise texts in ways appropriate to their content, and signpost this clearly to the reader.	Wr7 organise and present information, selecting appropriate material and making effective use of language, layout and illustration.	Wr6 integrate diverse kinds of information into a coherent account, using formal and impersonal language. Wr18 plan, organise, edit and present written work effectively, taking account of the time available and the range of possible formats.
Reasoning	Wr13 express and develop a personal view with clarity. Wr16 use a range of strategies to validate an argument.	Wr10 articulate abstract ideas or emotions for specified groups of readers. Wr13 present a counter-argument to a view that has been expressed, addressing weaknesses in the argument and offering alternatives.	Wr11 develop and signpost arguments in ways that make the logic clear to the reader and anticipate responses and objections. Wr17 record, develop and evaluate ideas through writing.

	YEAR 7	**YEAR 8**	**YEAR 9**
Enquiry		Wr20 experiment with different approaches to planning, drafting, checking and revising, judging their suitability for the task in hand.	Wr18 plan, organise, edit and present written work effectively, taking account of the time available and the range of possible formats.
Creative Thinking	Wr5 experiment with the visual and sound effects of language, including the use of imagery, alliteration, rhythm and rhyme. Wr6 use writing to explore and develop ideas.	Wr1 use language experimentally to explore ideas, emotions and imaginative experience. Wr 6 explore the visual and sound effects of language in a variety of poetic styles.	Wr1 entertain the reader by developing an imaginative or unusual treatment of familiar material. Wr3 write within the discipline of different poetic forms, identifying how form constrains and contributes to meaning.
Evaluation	Wr17 identify criteria for evaluating a particular text, object or event, present findings fairly and give a personal view. Wr21 find ways of testing the quality of written work.	Wr17 evaluate a process or product in relation to agreed criteria. Wr23 re-read work to anticipate the effect on the reader and revise style and structure, as well as accuracy, with this in mind.	Wr14 cite detailed textual evidence to justify critical judgements about texts and their overall impact. Wr16 review their own writing skills to recognise strengths and identify skills for further development.

21   References

Sheeran, Y and Barnes, D (1991) *School Writing*, OUP

Derewianka, B (1996) *Exploring the Writing of Genres*, UKRA

Wray, D and Lewis, M *Extending Literacy*, Routledge

Graves, D (1983) *Writing*, Heinemann

Draft Framework for English Years 7-9, NLP 2000

Technical Accuracy in writing in GCSE English: research findings, QCA 1999

Improving Writing at Key Stages 3 and 4, QCA 1999

Standards at Key Stage 3 English: Report on the 1999 national curriculum assessments for 14 year olds, QCA 2000

Standards at Key Stage 2 - English, Mathematics and Science: Report on the 1999 national curriculum assessments for 11-year-olds, QCA 2000

Standards at Key Stage 1 - English, Mathematics and Science: Report on the 1999 national curriculum assessments for 7-year-olds, QCA 2000

Teaching: High Status, High Standards Circular 4/98, DfEE 1998

The use of short extracts from the following books is gratefully acknowledged:

Waiting for the Rain by Sheila Gordon published by HarperCollins Educational, *Why the Whales Came* by Michael Morpurgo published by Collins Educational, *Harry Potter and the Philosopher's Stone* by J.K.Rowling published by Bloomsbury, *Skellig* by David Almond published by Hodder, *The Tulip Touch* by Anne Fine published by Puffin, *Junk* by Melvin Burgess published by Penguin Books and *Northern Lights* by Philip Pullman published by Scholastic Children's Books.

Jim Sweetman contributed Section 13, Working with Genre.

Aspects of this book draw on the findings of research funded by SCAA and the Qualifications and Curriculum Authority. The author and publishers acknowledge the contribution made by these agencies.

The article by Geraldine Hackett 'Boys close reading gap but still trail in writing' was published in the Times Educational Supplement on 8.10.99.